Makeover Magic

Stylish ideas to transform your
home on a budget

ANDREA MAFLIN

with Emma Cherry

CIMA BOOKS
London

First published in Great Britain in 2000
by Cima Books
32 Great Sutton Street
London EC1V 0NB
(0171) 245 0330

10 9 8 7 6 5 4 3 2 1

A CIP catalogue record for this book is available from the British Library

ISBN 1 903116 01 7 (hardback)
ISBN 1 903116 09 0 (paperback)

Project Editor: Kate Haxell

Designer: Suzanne Metcalfe-Megginson

Photography: Lucinda Symons and Brian Hatton

Co-designer: Emma Cherry

Stylist: Alistair Turnbull

Origination by Alliance Graphics, Singapore

Printed and bound by Tien Wah Press, Singapore

Contents

Introduction

Our home is usually a compromise between what we would like to have, and what we can afford. As such, it is sometimes not the place where we most want to be, which is a shame. Personally, I think of my home as a place where I can rest, a sanctuary from the hustle and bustle of the world outside. This is my place to rejuvenate, and I think everyone should have such a place.

With this in mind, I have looked at seven different rooms, each in dire need of help, in a variety of styles of property, from turn of the century to modern open-plan living. All the rooms present real problems for their owners, problems requiring solutions. From a completely empty room that had to house a living and an office space, to a dining room that had been used as a dumping ground, each room had it's own issues to be tackled. A narrow hall, tiny bathroom and a small garden were all challenging as space was so limited, while the bedroom and family room, although larger, were both extremely unsuccessful at the outset.

I started by talking to the owners of the properties to discover what they wanted from their space. I believe that you need to ask questions to find answers, as opposed to just guessing. I balanced the owner's wishes with what I thought was possible to do and in this way tried to extract the maximum potential from each of the rooms. I looked at the possible paint colours, the fabrics, the style, and feel of the room and these factors in turn suggested the projects. You can see how I worked through each room from the notes and samples shown on the Designer's Notebook pages.

I have made a wide range of projects for this book. Some are small in scale, such as the pleated lampshade in the bedroom, while some are large, such as the screen in the office/living room. I have concentrated on making everything simple to follow and satisfying to make. There are no specialist skills needed and few tools, and I have purposely kept the costs low. The projects team up with the Decorating Solutions; styling ideas, suggestions for very easy makes or variations on the projects, all of which will help to create a cohesive look in the room.

I hope that my solutions inspire you to look again at your own problem rooms. It only takes some imagination and a little time and money to really get your home to work for you.

The Family Room

Liveable Minimal

To a greater or lesser degree, a controlled chaos reigns in most family rooms. Once you accept that this is so, you can organize your space accordingly to suit everyone who needs to use the room. In days of old, children were seen and not heard and there was not a toy in sight. Nowadays it seems that children have taken over the world and in many family rooms there is not a grown-up thing to be found. I have re-designed this family room to create a balanced environment that accommodates both children and adults and encourages everyone to take collective responsibility for the living space.

This is a room that works for everyone: there are no childish primary colours and there is plenty of storage space. The colours and shapes are simple, clean and practical, allowing grubby fingers and grown-ups to live and play side-by-side.

Designer's Notebook

Whose room is this?

Peter and Sarah have two children and, as we know, children's lives and toys tend to take over, particularly in family rooms like this. Peter and Sarah never really had time to plan this room and now feel at a loss as to where to start. The room is uncomfortable, impractical and a constant frustration. They seem to spend their time tripping over toys, putting them away, then pulling them out again. There is not enough seating space for all the family, never mind any guests.

Colour and style

Peter and Sarah want a softer, almost country style in this room, something that feels peaceful and relaxed. However, they want it to be contemporary, not twee or rustic.

What do they want from the room?

The couple feel that the room lacks identity and order and is not used to its full potential. They want more places to sit and storage that is easy for children to use. They also want the storage to be fun, so that tidying up and keeping the room tidy is like playing.

Sarah does not want to use primary colours, which to her scream that children live here and adults take second place. She wants something altogether more sophisticated, but something that will not become grubby at the first hint of a child.

Possibilities and potential

In a way, a family room is the most difficult space to design successfully, because ultimately it is about compromise. You have to combine the ideal with the practical to make a room that offers function, comfort and aesthetic pleasure for everyone.

Conceal TV

Sofa needs attention

Solution: TV in storage cube

Before we started

Storage for toys needed

After we finished

Solution: new cushion covers and inexpensive throws to dress up sofa

Solution: coffee table also provides more storage

Colours for the insides of the MDF storage cubes

Colour for the outsides of the MDF storage cubes

Themes

Minimalism normally strikes fear in the heart of most families as it is not realistic, but the old rule of less is more is true. Most importantly, the room has to be practical and the space has to work for every one in the family. So we called this style Liveable Minimal, which put everyone's minds at rest. Listed below are the words I used as my inspiration.

Family

Storage

Fresh

Fun

Multi-functional

Practical

Play

Relaxation

Cement

Seating

The room is quite large with French windows leading out to the garden, so there is plenty of light. Storage is a major problem and the French windows mean that there is relatively little wall space to stand things against. The sofa is rather battered but it is comfortable and sound and Sarah feels that she can justify neither a new sofa or the expense of tailored loose covers. The ceiling is quite high but the current colour scheme visually lowers it, making the room look smaller. The tongue-and-grove below the dado is in good condition and is practical for the children.

Storage Cubes
These colour samples, shown above, are those I picked to paint the storage cubes in. As you can see in the detail, shown below, they all work well together and add a contemporary feel to the room.

Multi-level Storage
The lower cubes are perfect for all the children's belongings, while the higher cubes can be used to store and display Peter and Sarah's items out of a child's reach.

Curtain fabrics

Tab-top Curtains

These samples, right, show
the colours I dyed plain, white linen
in order to make the curtains,
shown left.

A good way to use up all the left-over scraps of fabric was to make different-sized laundry bags, which are brilliant for keeping assorted odds and ends in.

To create extra seating I covered solid foam cubes in fawn and soft moss-green suedette. These can be stacked out of the way and are comfortable for everyone, tall or small, to sit on. To make more storage, I sewed a pocket onto each cube to hold pens, pads, magazines and the ever-elusive television control.

Design solutions

I started with the walls and quickly got rid of the huge contrast between the top and bottom. I chose a sea-breeze blue below the dado rail and a fresh mint green above, with a rollered finish to distract from unsightly finger marks and to break up the colour.

The full-length windows needed dressing, so I made simple tab-top curtains in a light linen, to allow the light in. I dyed the curtains pale blue and added lime green self-pelmets to make them feel more substantial.

To revitalize the sofa I made cushion covers from fabric suedette and throws to protect the most vulnerable areas while remaining part of the intrinsic design. I had fun with colour, using sky blue with fennel green, and a bold rust in key places that might get scuffed or marked by resting heads.

Storage Bags

I made these bags, shown far right, from
left-over fabric from the sofa cushions. I
machine-embroidered motifs onto scraps of
the fabric used in the sofa throws, shown
right, then machined these onto the bags.

Wall paints

Paint Colours

I painted the tongue-and-
groove panelling in the fresh
blue and the wall above in
soft green, both shown left.
The pattern on the tiller
breaks up the colour,
as you can see on the right.

Next I tackled the storage problem and set about making a multitude of MDF cubes, all exactly the same size, which can be stacked in endless different ways. These allow full use of the available wall space. I painted the cubes in colours that complemented the rest of the design scheme, creating a co-ordinated look. With such plentiful storage there are no more excuses for messy toys and at the same time, there is plenty of room, at higher levels, for grown-up accessories such as pots, plants and vases. A television always seems to dominate a room and purpose-built furniture is very bulky, so I made a special cube to house the television and disguise it a little.

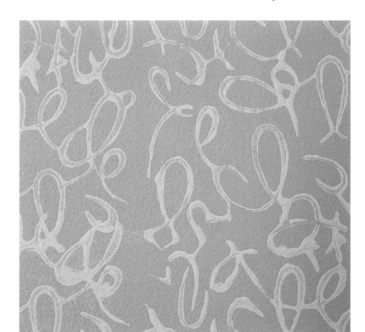

Rollered Wall Finish

This is such an easy way to make a plain, painted wall more
interesting, and the pattern helps to hide marks and scuffs.

Three of the cubes were mounted on castors to make a flexible coffee table that incorporated more storage space, this time for cushions that the children's friends can sit on to watch the television. Another fun idea was to paint the facing sides of each cube with blackboard paint for children, or adults, to draw and write on.

A project for the whole family was to make tealight and incense holders from cement coloured with fabric dye. This is good fun and they look and smell lovely when the candles and incense are alight.

The finished room suits all the family, is easy to keep tidy and can be transformed from a children's paradise to an adult heaven, by the flick of a switch and the lighting of a match.

Cube Seat

I made one of these seats in the pale green suedette, shown
below, with a fawn pocket, and the other seat in fawn with
a green pocket.

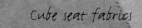

Cube seat fabrics

Cube Seat

Create extra seating for adults and children alike by covering foam cubes in suedette fabric. They provide great seating and can be stacked away when not in use. The shape echoes the storage cubes and so helps to integrate the seats into the design of the room.

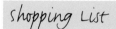

shopping List

50 x 50cm (20 x 20in) foam cube

six pieces of suedette measuring 54 x 54cm (21½ x 21½ in)

One piece of contrasting-coloured suedette measuring 20 x 20cm (8 x 8in)

sewing threads to match both fabrics

sewing machine and leather needle

Pins

Rotary cutter and cutting mat or scissors

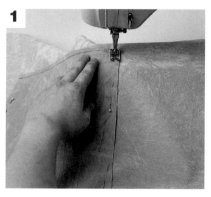

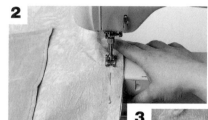

1. Turn under and machine a 1cm (½in) hem on one edge of the contrast suedette. Pin it to the centre of a main piece and topstitch round the raw edges to make the pocket.

2. Machine another main piece (which will be the top of the cube) to the top edge of the pocket piece, taking a 2cm (³/₄ in) seam allowance. Machine three other pieces in place around the top. Machine down all of the side edges. Machine one edge of the remaining (bottom) piece to one side piece.

3. Trim the seams on the machined edges to 0.5cm (¼in).

4. Fit the suedette cover over the foam cube. The easiest way to do this is to lay the top in place, then ruche up the machined edges and ease them down over the cube.

5. Turn the cube upside down and lay the bottom piece of suedette in place, aligning its raw edges with those of the remaining three unsewn sides.

6. Pin these bottom and side edges together and hand-stitch them closed using backstitch. Trim the seam allowance to 0.5cm (¼in).

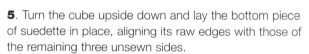

Cube Seat

I chose suedette fabric for these cubes as it doesn't fray, so the seams can be on the outside. However, you can make them from any other hard-wearing fabric. The method is the same, but you make the covers inside out and press seams open before putting the cover on the cube. Turn under the edges of the bottom piece and slip stitch them to the sides.

shopping List
Damp sand
Plastic washing-up bowl
Block of wood
Tealights
Jug
Cold water fabric dye
Water
Quick-drying cement
Palette knife

Tealight Holder

This is a project that all the family can help to make. However, you have to work fast once you have mixed the cement as it will live up to its name and start to dry very quickly.

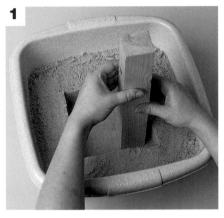
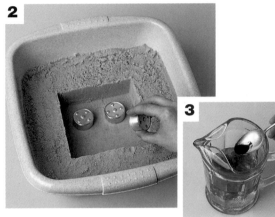

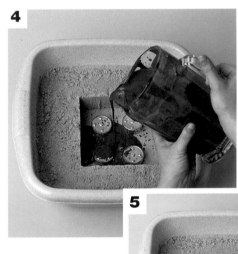

1. Put the damp sand in the washing-up bowl. Use the end of the block of wood to pack down the sand to make a mould, large enough to hold four tealights. You will have to pack the sand down in stages: make a shallow shape first, then gradually deepen it, working across the whole mould.
2. Place the tealights in position, upside down in the mould.
3. In the jug, mix a small amount of fabric dye into hot water. The amount you need will vary according to the colour you choose and the density you want, so you will have to experiment a little. Following the manufacturer's instructions, mix up the quick-drying cement, using the coloured water and

topping it up with plain water if necessary, making sure you have no lumps.
4. Pour the cement carefully into the mould, making sure that it doesn't run over onto the top of the sand.
5. Smooth the back of the cement with a palette knife and leave it to dry overnight. When it is dry, gently pull the tealight holder out of the mould and brush off any loose sand.

Tab-top Curtains

To give privacy without cutting out light, I made curtains from light linen, dyed to complement the walls. This colour-matching gives a cohesive look to the room. To make the curtains more of a feature in their own right, I added self-pelmets and bold patches.

Shopping List

For a pair of curtains:
Main fabric the length plus 6cm (2½ in) and 2½ times the width of the window

Iron

Tape measure

Pins

Sewing threads to match all fabrics

Sewing machine

Contrast fabric for the self-pelmet 2½ times the width of the window plus 8cm (3in) and one-fifth of the length of the window plus 8cm (3in)

Seven pieces of contrast fabric measuring 40cm (16in) by 6cm (2½ in) for the ties

Three or four pieces of contrast fabric measuring 26 x 34cm (10¼ x 13½ in) for the patches

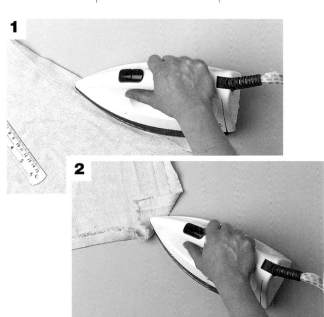

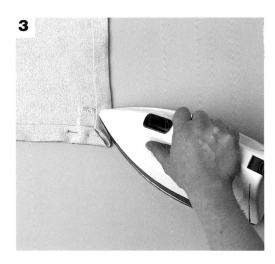

1. Press a double 2cm (³/₄ in) hem on both sides and the bottom edge of the main fabric. Leave the top edge raw.

2. To mitre the bottom corners, unfold the hems and press over a triangle at the corner. The base of the triangle should lie across the inner pressed hem line.

3. Re-fold the hems over the triangle to form a mitre. Pin and press.

4. Unfold the mitre and trim off the protruding tip of the triangle, then re-fold the mitre.

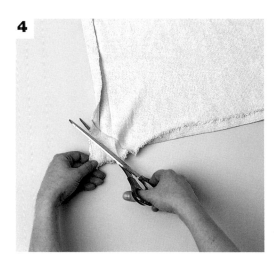

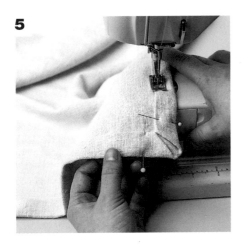

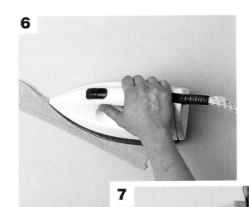

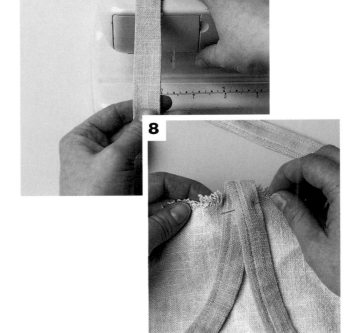

5. Machine all the hems, stitching close to the pressed edge. Make up the self-pelmet in exactly the same way, pressing double side and bottom hems and mitring the bottom corners. Again, the top edge should be left raw.

6. Press under a narrow hem on both long sides then both short sides of each tie.

7. Press the ties in half and topstitch each long side, close to the open edge.

8. Fold each tie in half and pin the fold to the back of the curtain, 1cm (1/2in) from the raw top edge.

9. Right side down, lay the self-pelmet on top of the folded ties on the back of the curtain, aligning the top raw edges. Machine through all layers, taking a 2cm (3/4in) seam allowance. Fold the pelmet to the right side of the curtain, hiding the raw edges and revealing the ties.

10. Decide where on the curtain you want the patches. Press under a narrow hem on each side, then pin and topstitch each patch in place.

Tab-top Curtains

These curtains are so practical as they are easy to take down and can be machine-washed whenever they need cleaning. If you want to make them without self-pelmets, simply mitre the top corners and hem the top edge and hand-sew the ties to the back of the top hem.

Shopping List

Two pieces of 8mm- (½in-) thick MDF measuring 40 x 40cm (16 x 16in)

Two pieces of 8mm- (½in-) thick MDF measuring 36 x 40cm (14 x 16in)

Drill

Wood screws

Wood filler

Sandpaper

PVA glue

Water

Paintbrush

Light shade of satinwood paint for the interior

Dark shade of satinwood paint for the exterior

Sponge roller and tray

Storage Cubes

Storage problems are easily solved with these multi-functional MDF cubes that can be stacked, added to and moved around. They work well if you keep all the outsides the same colour (a dark shade is best), and have fun with bright, funky tones inside.

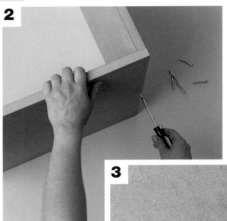

1. Drill three evenly spaced holes in two sides of the larger pieces of MDF.

2. Screw the larger pieces to the long ends of the smaller pieces to make a cube.

3. Fill the tops of the screw holes and any gaps with wood filler. Leave this to dry then sand it smooth. Seal the inside and outside of the cube with a solution of equal parts of PVA glue and water.

4. Using the paintbrush, paint the inside of the cube with two coats of the light shade of satinwood paint. Leave to dry between coats.

5. When the inside of the cube is dry, using the sponge roller, paint the outside with two coats of the darker shade of satinwood paint. Allow to dry between coats.

6. Very carefully roller around the front and back edges of the cube. Do not put too much paint on the roller or it will spread onto the inside of the cube. Leave to dry for at least eight hours.

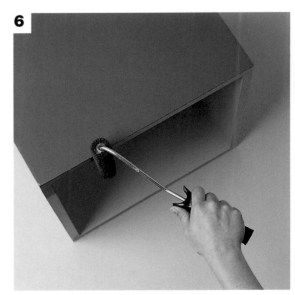

Storage Cubes

You can make storage cubes to almost any size you want, though you should use thicker MDF if they are to be very large, and thinner if they are to be very small. Paint the insides to complement the objects they will contain – as the cubes are separate you can always swap them around as you change the objects you have on display.

Sofa Cushions

These are a very practical way to refurbish a sofa that has seen better days but is still basically sound. Be adventurous with colour but practical with fabric, as it is going to take some wear and tear.

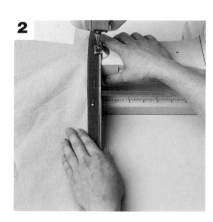

1. Place the plate on two front corners of the top and one of the two bottom pieces of suedette. Trim around it with the rotary cutter.

2. On a straight, long edge of one of the bottom pieces, turn under a 1cm ($\frac{1}{2}$in) hem to the wrong side. Lay one side of the Velcro close to the folded edge, pin and machine along both sides.

3. On the other bottom piece of suedette, turn a 1cm ($\frac{1}{2}$in) hem to the right side. Machine the other side of the Velcro to the right side of the fabric, positioning it close to the folded edge.

4. Right sides facing, pin and machine the border strip right around the edges of the top piece of suedette, taking a 2cm ($\frac{3}{4}$in) seam allowance.

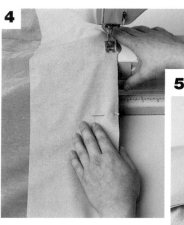

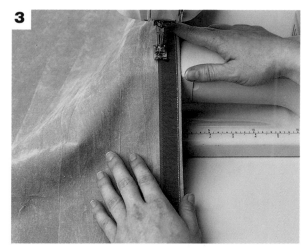

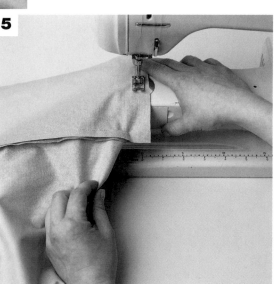

5. Velcro the two bottom pieces of the cover together. They should now measure the same as the top piece. Right sides facing, machine the bottom pieces, keeping them Velcro'd together, to the border. Reverse over the Velcro overlap twice to strengthen the seam. Undo the Velcro, turn the cover right-side out, insert the pad and do up the Velcro again.

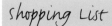

shopping List

For each cushion:
One piece of suedette fabric the length by the width of the pad plus 2cm ($\frac{3}{4}$in) all round for the top

Two pieces of suedette fabric the length of the pad plus 4cm ($1\frac{1}{2}$in) by the width plus 5cm (2in) for the bottom

Plate

Rotary cutter and cutting mat

2cm- ($\frac{3}{4}$in-) wide sew-on Velcro, the length of the pad

Pins

sewing thread

sewing machine

scissors

One piece of suedette fabric the depth of the pad plus 4cm ($1\frac{1}{2}$in) by the circumference plus 4cm ($1\frac{1}{2}$in) for the border

Sofa Cushions

To makeover this sofa I took off the original dark blue loose covers and made the new cushion covers to fit the pads. I dressed the rest of the sofa with throws (see Decorating Solutions, page 22 for more details). Alternatively, you could leave the loose covers on the body of the sofa, if they are not too tatty, and recover the cushions in a complementary fabric.

Decorating Solutions

Sofa Throws

A sofa in a family room is bound to get marked and stained, so the best solution is to cover it with washable throws. These are simple hemmed lengths of soft, plain fabric. I have added rectangles and borders in contrasting colours to introduce splashes of interest. You could make different throws for summer and winter to ring the changes in the room.

Incense Holder

This is made in the same way as the tealight holder (see page 14) but instead of tealights, push matchsticks into the sand to create holes in the cement for the incense sticks to slot into. A pair of pliers is a useful tool for pulling the matchsticks out of the dry cement. Incense comes in many varieties and is a wonderful way to perfume the air. Vanilla sticks are my personal favourites.

Storage Bags

Simple drawstring bags offer another easy way to store children's toys. You could embroider names or pictures of the toys that belong in them on the front, then everyone knows where the things belong and there are no excuses for leaving them lying around. Use left-over fabrics from the curtains, sofa cushions and cube seats and make as many bags as you need. Hang them from hooks or a peg-rail on the wall.

Coffee Table

I mounted three storage cubes onto castors to make a truly flexible coffee table cum storage and seating unit. The cubes can be pushed together or used separately as occasional tables. They can hold magazines, books or toys. I have stored cushions in one cube, which can be put on top of the cubes to make impromptu extra seating if you have extra visitors.

Blackboards

The coffee table also offers another idea for the child in all of us: your own secret picture gallery. Paint the facing sides of the coffee table cubes with blackboard paint, so that they can be pulled apart to be drawn on, yet the drawings can be hidden and the room made to look neater by pushing them back together. Make a storage bag (see opposite) for chalks and a rubber and hang it near to hand.

Rollered Wall Finish

Patterned rollers are the simplest way to give your walls an interesting finish. They are available from good DIY or paint shops and come in a range of patterns. You paint the wall a base colour and allow it to dry. Then pour a little paint in another colour into the roller tray, roll the patterned roller through it and then onto the wall. You can create wonderful effects by painting the two coats in complementary colours.

The Dining Room

Modern Glamour

Staying in is the new going out, or so they say! Entertaining is all about creating an environment in which you and your guests can enjoy food, drink and convivial company. It should be an experience that heightens all the senses and makes everyone feel special and relaxed. Too often the dining room is ignored or only used for formal occasions, but a meal is one of the most enjoyable necessities in life. Therefore, a dining room should not just be somewhere you eat; it should represent your style and be as comfortable and pleasant to sit in as any other room in your home.

Create a dining room that you are proud to share and enjoy. The scene is set and your guests are about to arrive. Everything is ready for a wonderful evening of stories and laughter.

Designer's Notebook

Appliquéd Cushion
I used suedette fabric, samples of which are shown right, to make cushions, shown far right.

Cushion fabrics

Whose room is this?
This room belongs to Stuart and Sarah, who moved in two years ago. They both work full-time, and only recently got started on turning their house into their home. The dining room has been a dumping ground while they've been working on the rest of the house, so things can only get better.

What do they want from this room?
Stuart and Sarah love entertaining and want to combine the special feeling of dining out in a restaurant with the relaxed atmosphere of being at home with friends. They also want to use the room on a daily basis, so it needs to be practical and comfortable as well as glamourous, with plenty of storage for their china and glassware.

Potential and possibilities
Initially it was difficult to see the room's potential as it was full of things that didn't belong there, like the washing machine.Once we had cleared it, however, we could see that it is actually quite big. Being a modern house, the ceilings are quite low and there are no period features. It has quite good natural light but only from one window. The design scheme has to complement the oak floor, as Stuart really likes it.

Design Solutions
To open the space up I decided to paint the walls with two warm colours in roughly the same tone: an earthy khaki and a soft mole. To add interest I

Colour and style
Stuart and Sarah definitely want to get away from magnolia. They love colour and sparkle, but they don't want anything 'mad'.

Walls need colour and texture

Solution: coloured voile draped at window

Solution: painted and glazed walls in two colours

simple window treatment needed

Before we started

After we finished

Owners want to keep floor as it is

Solution: seat cushions make metal chairs comfortable

Leaf Motifs
I appliquéd simple leaf shapes, also cut from suedette fabric, in different arrangements onto each cushion.

textured the walls by painting them with a base coat of emulsion and then dragging a glaze over the top.

The dining table that the couple already owned was a lovely shape, but the surface had seen better days. To give it a facelift I painted the tabletop to match the walls and then I wood-grained it with a darker glaze: a stunning effect with a twist, as I used unusual colours rather than traditional wood colours. Stuart and Sarah already had some interesting metal chairs that I

Wood-grained Table
The wood-grained effect was applied in a dark-coloured glaze so that it shows up well on the paler background.

Wood-grained finish

The original dining table

Beaded Table Mats

Silver beads, shown right, were woven into a strip, which was used to trim the table mats, shown far right.

re-sprayed with silver enamel paint. Cushion pads are an effective way to transform chairs, and make them more comfortable, so I made some from suedette fabric appliquéd with powder-blue leaf motifs.

To store, and display, china and glasses I made some simple storage cubes. They were made from MDF and painted in soft lilac and stone to complement the walls. These can be stacked and moved around easily, so they provide flexible storage.

Lighting is always important and although there is plenty of natural light from the window during the day, careful thought needs to go into the evening light in this room. There is no central light, so I decided to use wall lights. Rather than hide them, as a lot of us do, I chose to make a feature of them and make them look like pieces of art. Stuart and Sarah took some photographs which I had enlarged and laminated and then I hung them from brackets mounted straight onto the walls.

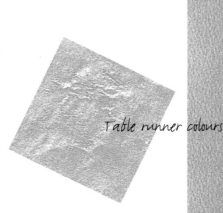

Table runner colours

Gilded Glass Runner

Silver leaf, shown above, and turquoise paint, shown right, combine beautifully in the table runner, shown left.

Wood-grain colours

Wood-grain colours

Shown left are the pale paint colour and the dark glaze colour I used on the dining table, shown below.

I bought some inexpensive white table mats and dyed them to match the leaf motifs on the cushion pads. Beads are making a comeback and a beaded trim is the ideal way to add a touch of glamour to any setting, table or otherwise.

Glass and gilding also add to the glamourous theme and a glass table runner with carefully chosen motifs made a wonderful centrepiece for the table.

Brushed Paint Finish

Shown left are samples of the wall colours and finish. Half of each sample has been painted in plain paint and the other half textured with the glaze over the paint.

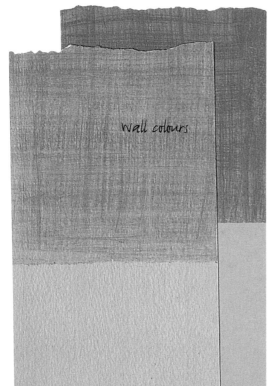

Wall colours

Storage Cubes

Tall enough to hold long-stemmed glasses and wide enough for the largest dinner plates, these cubes provide ideal storage for a dining room.

Appliquéd Cushions

Metal chairs can be uncomfortable to sit on, so cushions are a must in the dining room. I made these in two colours, so you can change the look a little by turning over the cushions.

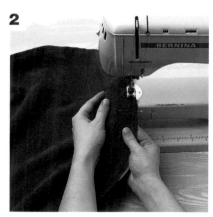

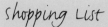

Shopping List

45cm (18in) round, feather cushion pad

Paper for making patterns

Scissors

50cm (20in) square of grey and of burgundy suedette fabric for the top and bottom

150 x 10cm (59 x 4in) of grey suedette fabric for the border

Pins

Sewing thread

Sewing machine and leather needle

Leaf motifs (see page 124)

20 x 20cm (8 x 8in) of sky-blue suedette fabric for the appliqué motifs

Burgundy embroidery thread

Long, sharp sewing needle

1. Cut a paper pattern 2cm ($^3/_4$ in) larger all round than the cushion pad. Pin the pattern to the suedette and cut one circle from the grey suedette and one circle from the burgundy suedette. For the border, cut a strip of grey suedette 4cm ($1^1/_2$ in) longer than the circumference and 4cm ($1^1/_2$ in) wider than the depth of the cushion pad.

2. As suedette doesn't fray, and to make the cushions a little different, I made them up with the seams on the outside. This also makes life a lot easier when it comes to finishing off the cushions. First, wrong sides facing, machine the border strip around the bottom section of the cushion, taking a 2cm ($^3/_4$ in) seam allowance. Machine the short ends together.

3. Trace or photocopy the leaf motifs on page 124 and cut them out to make templates. Pin the templates to the sky-blue suedette and cut out the motifs.

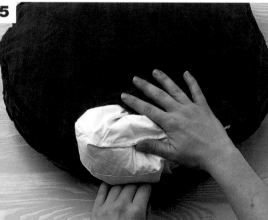

4. Position the motifs on the cushion top and pin them in place. With the burgundy embroidery thread and the long, sharp needle, sew the motifs to the cushion using running stitch.

5. Wrong sides facing, machine the cushion top to the border strip, leaving a 15cm (6in) opening. Push the pad into the cover and make sure it is evenly distributed. Hand-sew the opening closed.

Appliquéd Cushions

Suedette is only available in a limited colour range, so to suit
my colour scheme for this dining room I dyed white suedette
grey (for the tops of the cushions) and blue (for the appliquéd
motifs). This is easily done in the washing machine with fabric
dye; just follow the dye manufacturer's instructions.

Brushed Paint Finish

Once you start to explore colours and types of paints you will find lots to chose from. This simple technique and easy-to-follow recipe has marvellous effect, creating softly textured walls which are not overpowering and are very easy to live with.

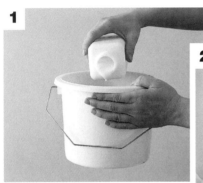

1. Make up the glaze by mixing six parts of acrylic classic paint medium (see Suppliers), six parts of water and one part of emulsion. The mixture should have the consistency of single cream; add more water if it is too thick. You need to make up approximately 3.5 litres (6¼ pints) of glaze to cover a 20sqm (20sqyd) wall. Make up the quantity of glaze you require in each colour.

2. Paint the walls with the emulsion paints. You will probably need two coats. Leave to dry.

3. If possible, it is best to get a friend to help you with the next steps as you need to work fast. Working in vertical sections about 1m (1yd) wide, brush the glaze on and then drag the wide, flat paintbrush vertically through the glaze.

4 Drag the brush horizontally through the glaze to create an almost woven effect.

5. Finally, drag the brush vertically through the glaze once again. If one of you brushes on the glaze and the other drags it, you will be able to work quickly enough to keep the edge of the paint wet, so that the next section blends in. In this way you can avoid unsightly hard lines.

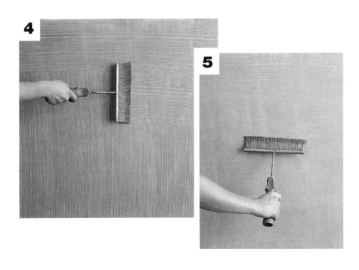

Wood-grained Table

What do you do when your budget is over-stretched but you need to transform your old table to suit your new room? A simple, and very affordable, solution is to paint it.

1

Glaze recipe: mix four parts of acrylic scumble glaze (see Suppliers), four parts of water and one part of emulsion to the consistency of single cream. Add more water if necessary as the glaze must be translucent.

2

2. Brush the glaze onto the surface. Pull the wood-grainer across the glaze, using a rocking motion to create the wood-grain effect. You can work in stripes in one direction and then go back and fill in the plain areas by wood-graining in the opposite direction. If it doesn't look right the first time, wipe off the wet glaze and start again. Leave to dry.

1. Sand the table top and wipe it down with a damp cloth first and then a dry cloth. Paint the entire table top evenly with the base colour. You may need two coats. Leave to dry for several hours.

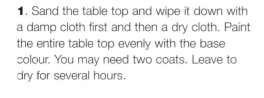

3

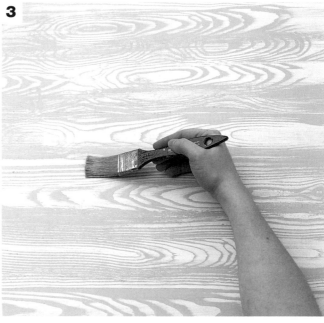

3. Seal the table with at least two coats of acrylic varnish.

Gilded Glass Runner

A table runner is a practical, and suitably glamourous, alternative to an untidy row of mats in the centre of the table. If you're only going do one project for your dining room, let it be this one.

1. Photocopy the motifs on page 124 and place them under the glass. Walk right round the glass and make sure that you're happy with the balance of the design you have created from all angles. Then stick the motifs in place with masking tape. With the acrylic size, trace the motifs directly onto the glass. If you make a mistake, carefully wipe it away with a damp cloth. Leave the size to become tacky; this should take about five to ten minutes.

2. Lay a sheet of silver transfer leaf onto the size and rub the paper backing gently to ensure that the leaf sticks.

3. Carefully peel the paper backing away. Some motifs may need several sheets of transfer leaf to cover them. If there are bits missing, simply place another sheet of transfer leaf on top

and repeat the process. If you have missed painting any areas with the size, you can brush more on and repeat steps 2 and 3.

4. Leave the runner to dry for half-an-hour then brush away any excess leaf pieces with the soft brush.

5. For this step you need to wear a protective breathing mask and work in a well-ventilated room. Put down paper or old newspaper to protect the work surface. With the enamel paint, spray the glass evenly, covering all the silver leaf. It is better to spray a couple of thin coats as opposed to one thick coat, as this will run. Allow to dry. Brush oil-based varnish over the paint to seal it and allow to dry overnight.

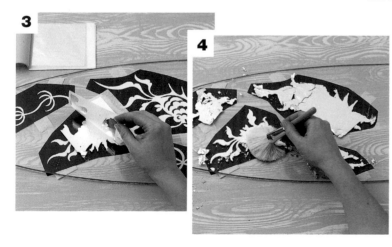

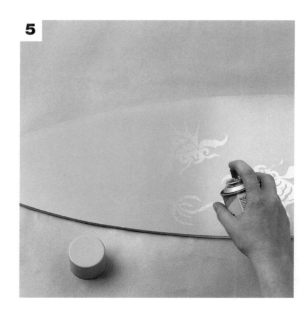

Gilded Glass Runner

This is a practical project as all the work is underneath the glass and is, therefore, protected. You can, of course, use any motifs and there are a variety of metal leaf transfers to choose from. If gilding doesn't appeal to you, try painting a piece of acrylic with acrylic paints. Alternatively, if you like sewing, you could appliqué motifs onto a fabric table runner.

Beaded Table Mats

Dye white mats to the colour of your choice, add beaded trims and you have in your possession objects of great beauty. They will add that touch of sparkle, which evokes glamour and style, to your table.

Shopping List

For four mats:
Four fabric table mats
700g (1lb 9oz) glass beads
Beading needle
scissors
Reel of beading thread to match the beads
sewing needle
Reel of sewing thread to match the mats

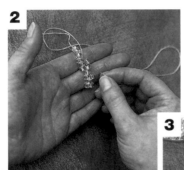

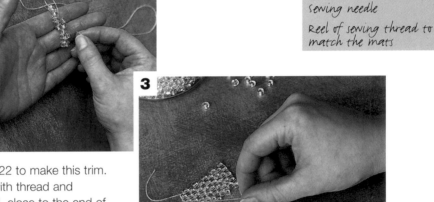

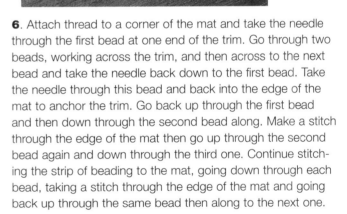

1. Follow the beading diagram on page 122 to make this trim. To get started, thread a beading needle with thread and double it. Slip a bead over the needle and, close to the end of the thread, tie a firm double knot round the bead. This will be bead number 1 in the diagram.

2. Thread on ten more beads and then start to work back up the row, adding more beads as illustrated.

3. Continue building up the rows of beads and the strip will start to take shape.

4. When you have only about 10cm (4in) of thread left, cut it off close to the needle, Thread up the needle again and tie all the ends together in a tight single knot. Trim the loose ends.

5. When you have made a strip of beading long enough to run down the side of the mat, finish the strip off by weaving the thread in and out of several beads. Make a loop round the thread between two beads, take the needle through the loop and pull it up tightly. Trim off the thread.

6. Attach thread to a corner of the mat and take the needle through the first bead at one end of the trim. Go through two beads, working across the trim, and then across to the next bead and take the needle back down to the first bead. Take the needle through this bead and back into the edge of the mat to anchor the trim. Go back up through the first bead and then down through the second bead along. Make a stitch through the edge of the mat then go up through the second bead again and down through the third one. Continue stitching the strip of beading to the mat, going down through each bead, taking a stitch through the edge of the mat and going back up through the same bead then along to the next one.

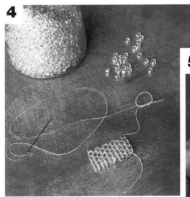

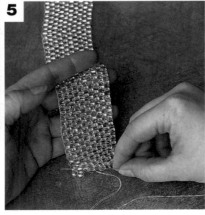

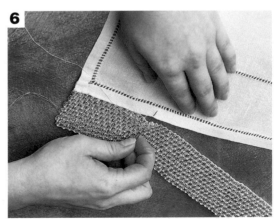

Beaded Table Mats

Table mats are sometimes seen as old-fashioned. However, if you dye plain fabric mats to match other furnishings in the room and add this glittering beaded trim, they become both contemporary and stylish additions to your table.

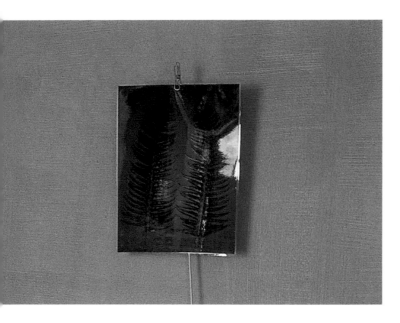

Decorating Solutions

Photographic Wall Lights

These lights, or more correctly, light covers, are simply laminated colour copies of photographs attached to wall brackets. Choose abstract images in colours to suit your room, or favourite scenes, or even family or friends. Ensure that the wall brackets you use hold the laminate far enough away from the bulb so that it doesn't get scorched.

Storage Cubes

Finding enough storage is a never-ending problem that I'm sure we all suffer from. If everything is hidden away in cupboards then we can never quite remember what we have, and if items have no proper home, the room looks messy and things get broken. These storage cubes (see page 18 for instructions on how to make them) solve all these problems. They can be stacked to suit any available space and enable you to both put things away and still see what you've got.

Painted Chairs

Stuart and Sarah bought these metal chairs in a second-hand shop and really liked them. However, they were quite rusty so I rubbed them down with wire wool and transformed them with a coat of silver enamel paint. The finishing touches were the appliquéd cushions (see page 30 for instructions).

Printed Pots

These inexpensive, plain pots were mono-printed in sky-blue paint to co-ordinate with the motifs on the appliquéd cushions. I used an oil-based paint so that the pots can be washed, but they can't go in the dishwasher. Mono-printing is simple to do (see page 111 for instructions) and can be used to liven up almost anything: just remember to choose the right paint for the job.

Mosaic Mirror

The wall next to the window in this dining room was quite dark, so I hung a mirror there to reflect light. This mirror was made the same way as the one in the hall (see page 62 for instructions), the only difference being that it is smaller. An alternative to a mirror tiled border would be to use coloured ceramic mosaic tiles.

Beaded Napkin Rings

To make your table extra special you can create your own napkin rings by following the steps for the beaded table mat trim (see page 36 for instructions) and simply joining the ends to form a circle. Make napkin rings to match the table mats, or you could use different-coloured beads to create stripes or even checks.

The Office/ Living Room

Retro Futuristic

Modern lifestyles mean that often we must be flexible in the ways that we live and work. More and more of us are choosing to work for ourselves, and often this means working from our homes. The home and office can, however, spill over into each other and we find ourselves with no space for either. It is important to create physical and mental space, with clear boundaries that also allow flexibility. Remember that the room is still part of a home and avoid creating a space that takes no risks, encourages nothing and says little about who lives and works there.

Designer's Notebook

Whose room is this?

Paul and Emma have recently got married and have just moved into a studio flat in a converted Victorian light-industrial building. They have done absolutely nothing to the place yet and, although they both have good ideas, they need guidance, otherwise their interest in 20th-century design will probably mean that they will end up with a small museum, rather than a home.

What do they want from the room?

Both Paul and Emma are involved in different aspects of interior and television design and plan to run their businesses from home. There are not enough rooms for a separate office so the main room will have to operate both as an office and as their living space.

They are both very much up to date with current interior fashions but they have very a clear sense of their own style. They like open space and geometric designs and cannot resist a 20th-century classic. They have, for example, an interesting 1950s sideboard, which needs refurbishing and which they would like to incorporate into the room.

Possibilities and potential

The room has very high ceilings and full-length windows that open onto a faux balcony. The view, however, is not inspiring. The room is high-ceilinged, light and airy and lends itself to a minimalist approach, which complements the clean and simple lines that both Paul and Emma favour.

They want colours that encourage both creativity and hard work, while also enabling calm and relaxation. The colour scheme will be made up of sophisticated white

Colour and style

The room will remain primarily a minimalist white, but will be softened and divided with blocks of strong colour.

Consider storage on this wall

White walls need breaking up with other colours

Before we started

This should be the living area as it is near the kitchen

solution: shelving with built-in lights

After we finished

solution: refurbish sideboard for storage

sideboard colour

1950s Sideboard

I chose cherry-red gloss paint and a rich teak wood stain to revitalize this sideboard. The only ugly things about it were the door handles, but the drilled holes replaced these.

and brown, suggesting simplicity, while rich red promotes inspiration and activity. A milky blue offers a peaceful aspect. The other colours that will pull the palette together will be fawn, rust and olive green to keep everyone's feet firmly on the ground, and soft purple, a wild card to remind us all that this should not be taken too seriously.

Design solutions

I decided to leave the walls primarily white and use strong colours just on small areas, an arrangement that suits Paul and Emma's personal style. The rich red around the entrance to the kitchen serves to define it

Drilled Flower Vase

I continued the drilled-holes theme by using them to make a simple wooden box into a vase. The box conceals glasses of water that the flowers are pushed into.

Vase colour

Themes

Retro Futuristic taps into the constant return to the recent past, yet also allows modern thoughts on colour and space to influence the many different moods required for balanced living and working. I used the following words as my reference points.

Living/working

Three-dimensional

Inspiring

Artworks

Light

Space

Wool

Felt

Acrylic

PVC

Friendly/minimal

Drilling

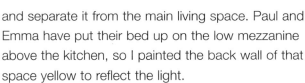

Multi-media Screen

A screen is a brilliant device for dividing up a room as it can be moved around so easily. However, I wanted this one to be more than just a divider: I wanted it to be multi-functional as well as multi-media.

and separate it from the main living space. Paul and Emma have put their bed up on the low mezzanine above the kitchen, so I painted the back wall of that space yellow to reflect the light.

The end of the main room next to the kitchen will be the living space, so I had a large shelf unit, which incorporates two lights, built to go on the wall. Below this hang two of Paul's paintings, and below them stands the 1950s sideboard, given a new lease of life with a coat of cherry-red paint and re-modelled doors. A tiny element of work has crept into the living space in

the form of files stored in the sideboard. To keep their files separate, the couple use a colour system: the blue files are Emma's and the orange ones, Paul's.

The sofa and armchairs are more 1950s' finds from a second-hand shop and are in good condition. They did not need re-covering but I introduced a knitted patchwork throw to add more colour.

some kind of room divider needed

solution: desk folds away to make space

solution: screen hides office area

Windows need dressing to create privacy and hide view

Before we started

Flexible work station at this end of the room

solution: fabric banners and frosted windows give privacy

After we finished

Wall colours

The office end of the room naturally focuses around the desk, but I devised two ways of minimizing its impact on the living space. If Paul and Emma are entertaining on a big scale, the desk can easily be taken apart and folded completely flat to be stored under the bed. On a day-to-day basis, a screen can be moved in front of the desk to banish work for the evening. The screen itself has one felt-covered cork panel that can be used as a pin-board, and another panel with a sheet of acrylic attached to each side with mirror fixings for Emma and Paul to stick their endless notes and reminders. The third panel is woven from strips of PVC, into which more notes or business cards can be pushed.

The windows look out onto a courtyard and I really wanted to mask the view a little without cutting out too much light. So, I frosted the bottom half of the central windows, leaving a pattern of clear squares, and hung narrow silk banners at each side window. I mono-printed the banners with circles of colour.

Wall Colours

Using blocks of colour in a mainly white space adds warmth and interest while still keeping a minimal feel. I chose rich, strong colours that really stand out and call attention to themselves.

The finished space reflects Paul and Emma's interests and lifestyle. It is flexible enough for them both to run their businesses from and to meet clients in, to entertain their friends and families and, very importantly, to relax and live in as a home.

Knitted Throw

The soft pile of chenille wool gives an added luxury to anything knitted from it. This throw, with its knitted bobbles or embroidered knots, is so textural that it is impossible not to touch it.

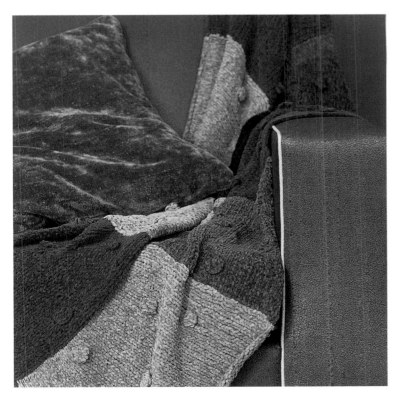

Wool colours

Frosted Windows

A great alternative to nets for retaining privacy, hiding an ugly outlook and letting in light is to use frosting spray. Mask off transparent squares, or any other shape, for the best effect.

shopping List

Low-tack sticky-backed plastic
Cutting mat
Craft knife
Metal ruler
Masking tape
Spirit level
Layout paper or newspaper
Protective breathing mask
Frosting spray

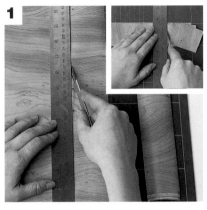

1

2

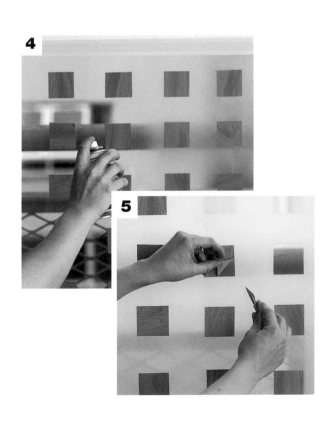

3

1. Cut out 5 x 5cm (2 x 2in) squares of sticky-backed plastic on a cutting mat, using the metal ruler and craft knife.
2. Measure and mark out the spacing on the window with the masking tape. Peel the backing paper off the sticky-backed plastic and stick the squares onto the glass.
3. Using the spirit level, check that the squares are in straight horizontal and vertical lines. Mask off the surrounding areas with tape and layout paper or newspaper. This is important as the spray does tend to drift about a bit.
4. Ensure that the room is well-ventilated and, wearing a protective breathing mask, spray the frosting evenly over the window and allow to dry. It is better to apply several thin coats rather than one thick one, as the spray can drip if it is too thick.
5. Immediately remove the squares of plastic by carefully lifting an edge of each square with the craft knife and peeling them off.

4

5

Multi-media Screen

An old idea that offers an ideal way to change the shape and look of your living/working space. Be brave with colours and materials to make it really dynamic and interesting, giving a strong sense of the past coming face-to-face with the future.

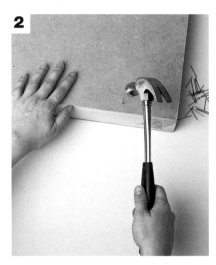

1. Make up three rectangular frames by screwing two long lengths of battening to each end of two short lengths.
2. Using panel pins, nail an MDF panel to each side of two of the frames.
3. Take one of the MDF-panelled frames and glue the cork tiles to both sides of it.
4. Trim off any excess cork with a craft knife and a metal ruler.

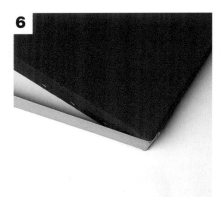

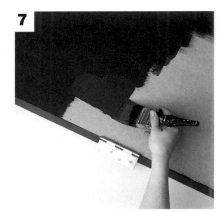

5. Lay the felt over the cork and, using the staple gun, staple the felt to the sides of the frame. Trim off any excess felt close to the line of staples.

6. Cut a 220 x 6cm (82 x 2$\frac{1}{2}$in) strip of PVC. Staple one end to the bottom of the felt-covered panel, stretch it up the side of the panel and staple it at the top. This will cover the staples holding the felt in place. Repeat this on the other side of the frame. Set this panel aside.

7. Paint both sides of the second MDF-covered panel and leave it to dry.

8. It is best to have the acrylic cut to size and the holes drilled, but you can do these yourself with a metal drill bit. Lay the acrylic over the painted panel, mark the positions of the holes on the paint and drill six holes in the frame. Using mirror screws, screw the plastic to each side of the panel.

9. Make up the woven panel on the uncovered frame. Cut twenty-four lengths of PVC measuring 5cm (2in) by 210cm (82in) and eighty lengths measuring 5cm (2in) by 70cm (28in).

10. Start by stapling twelve of the long, vertical strips to the edge of one short end of the frame. Each strip should butt up to the next without overlapping. Pull the PVC taut across the

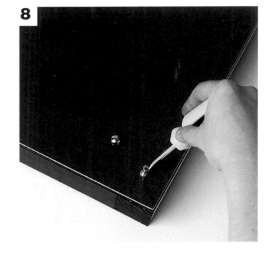

length of the frame and staple the other end of each strip to the other short end of the frame.

11. Staple one end of forty of the short, horizontal strips to the edge of one long side of the frame. They should butt up as before. Weave the short lengths through the long lengths, going under and over on alternate rows. Staple the other end of each short length to the other long edge of the frame. Repeat the process on the other side of the frame with the remaining twelve long strips and forty short strips. Screw hinges to each panel to make up the screen.

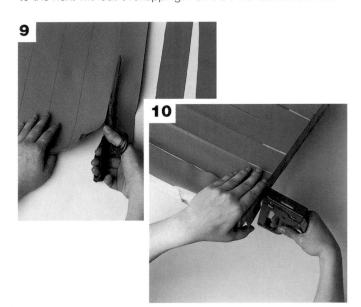

Multi-media Screen

Not only is this screen multi-media, it is also designed to be multi-purpose. Pin notes, receipts and mementoes to the felt-covered cork panel; use the acrylic-covered panel to hold the ubiquitous sticky-backed notes and tuck business cards and invitations into the weave of the PVC panel. Decide on your own needs and dream up a surface to suit them.

Simple Lamp

Here a truly modern material is used to great effect, with an interesting image or photograph to give it an edge. The beauty of this lamp is that you can change the image whenever you want.

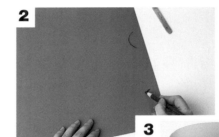

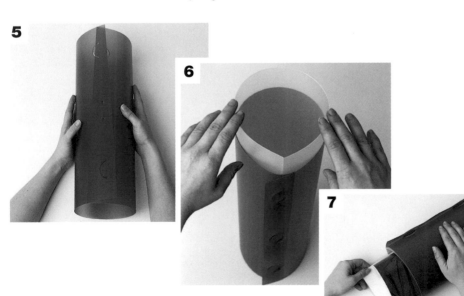

1. Measure out and cut a 45 x 40cm (18 x 16in) rectangle in the purple polyprop and a 40 x 40cm (16 x 16in) square in the white polyprop.

2. On the purple polyprop, draw three crescent shapes with the chinagraph pencil, evenly spaced down one short side of the rectangle.

3. Bring the two edges together and trace the crescents out on the other edge of the rectangle.

4. Carefully cut out the crescents with a sharp craft knife. Also cut a small semi-circle in the lower edge of the purple and the white polyprop, close to the crescents, for the electric cable.

5. Roll the purple polyprop into a tube and hook the crescents inside one another to hold the lamp together.

6. Roll up the white polyprop and slide it into the purple tube.

7. Roll up the laminated photograph and slide it inside the white polyprop. Set the lamp over a base, with the electric cable running through the cut-out semi-circle.

Simple Lamp

This really must be the simplest project to make in this book.
You just need to be able to cut straight and curved lines. As it
is so easy to make, you can be bold with colour and imagery;
they won't make the project any harder. Choose a coloured
polyprop to complement your room and an image that will
stand out well when the light shines through it.

1950s Sideboard

Shopping List

Sandpaper
Cloth
Wood stain or varnish
Red emulsion paint
Cherry red gloss paint
Paintbrush
Pen and ruler
Drill
10mm (½in) wood drill bit

With a little imagination and lateral thinking this tatty sideboard has been transformed into a fantastic fusion of old and new. It also beautifully fulfils its new function as a combined stationery cupboard and filing cabinet.

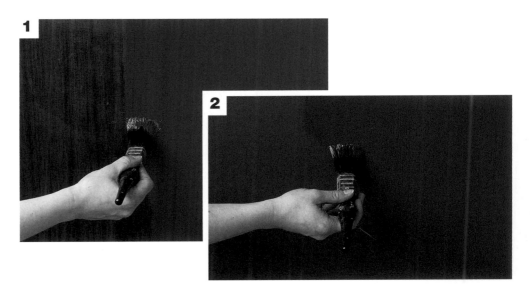

1. Prepare the sideboard by sanding off any varnish and wiping down the wood. Decide which parts of the sideboard you want to paint and which will remain as wood. Stain or re-varnish the wooden areas. Paint the remaining sanded wood with red emulsion and leave it to dry.
2. Paint the primed areas with two coats of gloss paint.

3. Take off the doors and draw a 1cm (½in) grid on the back in pen. Leave a border of 4cm (1½in) at the top and sides and 4.5cm (1¾in) at the bottom. Mark the junction of every fourth square with a dot to indicate where the holes will be.
4. Drill the holes and sand the edges smooth. Prime and paint the doors as before and re-hang them.

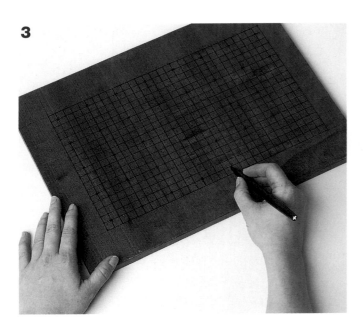

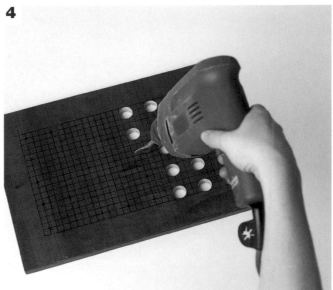

1950s Sideboard

Next time you go into a second-hand furniture shop, try to look at pieces with a fresh eye. They may be awful as they are but, if they are structurally sound, do they have potential? Little touches (like the drilled doors in this cupboard) can enliven and modernize a boring piece of furniture. And, of course, satin or gloss paint is the perfect way to cover cheap or stained wood.

Knitted Throw

This is a knitting project which is truly satisfying, simple to do and very touchable. The bobbles or French knots really make it three-dimensional. Start small and you can always add more squares.

Shopping List

Chenille wool in rust, fawn, olive green and aubergine

5mm (No. 6/US 8) knitting needles

Large darning needle

Pins

Matching sewing threads

Sewing needle

1. Following the pattern on page 122, knit as many squares as you require.

2. If you prefer not to knit the bobbles, then you can embroider French knots instead. To make these, thread a large darning needle with two strands of the chenille wool. Pull the needle through from the back of the square. Wrap the wool twice round the needle and pull the knot up tightly. Take the needle through to the back and fasten off. Make the knots either in a pattern or randomly over each square.

3. Lay out the squares and plan the arrangement of the colours in the throw before you start sewing it all together. Right sides facing, and with the rows of knitting at right angles to one another, sew the squares together. Use matching thread and a firm backstitch.

One of the bobbles shown below is knitted and the other embroidered. As you can see, they look just the same, so it really is up to you as to which you use.

Knitted Throw

This throw is a perfect project for beginners to knitting as you can simply knit plain squares and embroider them with French knots. If you are a more experienced knitter you may like to include cabled or intarsia panels as well. Choose your favourite designs and adapt them to suit squares. If you hate knitting, consider making a traditional knot-quilted throw instead.

Decorating Solutions

Printed Window Banners

Mono-printing circles onto stripes of fabric requires a bit of planning but the finished result is marvellous. Choose a plain material with a pleasing texture (I used dupion silk) and print it in colours to match other furnishings in the room. (See page 111 for instructions for mono-printing onto fabric.) If you are feeling adventurous, print cushion covers or a throw in the same way.

Shelf Light

The lovely soft light shining through the opalescent acrylic lamps at each end of this shelf complements the space and gives it a futuristic feel. In addition, there is plenty of space to store books, display objects and hold flowers. Though the shelf looks complicated to make, it is basically only an MDF box with two pieces of acrylic slotted in place at each end. Sand, fill and paint the MDF and house a lamp in each acrylic box. You must also cut vents in the MDF to let heat from the lamps escape.

Coloured Filing System

When two people are working in a fairly small space it is really important to organize paperwork well, or chaos will ensue. This system involves covering files and books in different-coloured papers so that each person can instantly recognize what is theirs. As a bonus, the files look so attractive that they don't need to be hidden away in a cabinet.

Wood-grained Mirror

Mirrors are wonderful, as they reflect the light around the room and create the illusion of space. Have some fun with the wood-grain technique (see page 33 for instructions) and make a fantastic mirror frame. You don't need to use wood-like colours; try graining in purple or lime green for a contemporary look, or muted crimson or gold for a dramatic touch.

Drilled Flower Vase

While you're drilling holes in your sideboard doors, why not get some MDF, drill some more holes and create the framework for a vase. Simply put small glasses inside and fill them with water and fragrant flowers. Colour is particularly important for flower containers as shades that are too strong will dominate the blossoms. This blue is fresh and relaxing, perfect for lilies. A soft green or warm gold would also work well.

Flat-pack Desk

Made from five rectangles of MDF, this pack-away table is painted in a deep inky blue, which suggests serious activity and simplicity of style. It is large enough to hold a computer, phone and work in progress and it can double up as a dining table or a work table too. When you want more space it only takes a minute to take the top off, fold the hinged legs flat and stow the whole thing under the bed.

The Hall

Contemporary Classic

Entrances and exits are unpredictable, you
never know exactly who is going back and
forth. However, they are the first and last
point of contact, the doorway to your home,
and should create a good impression.
Halls are often neglected in terms of
decorating, as they are a difficult room to
get right. It is a real juggling act to create a
practical place where one can leave keys
and correspondence or messages, as well
as making it warm and welcoming.
Make it clear where things live, use colours
that work in all lights and at all times of the
year and add personal touches to integrate
the room with the rest of your home.

Keeping the colours clean and co-ordinated
opens out the space. The colourful tassels,
which appear on items throughout the room,
are a softening touch.

Designer's Notebook

Wall Panels
I chose vibrant colours
that reflect those in the
stained-glass window and
door for the wall panels.

Whose room is this?

Andrew and Celia have two children, both of whom are at school. They moved here about 18 months ago and are in the process of completely refurbishing the house. Andrew is an architect and Celia is a university lecturer with a particular interest in plants and herbs.

What do they want from the room?

Andrew is Danish and, being an architect, has very clear ideas about design. He likes simple, clean lines and the decoration of the rest of the house reflects this. His aim is to remain true to the period of the house as far as possible without compromising personal style. The couple see the hall as the gateway to their home and they want it to be welcoming and inviting to friends, family and clients alike. In addition, it must fulfil certain needs, such as having places for keys, stationery, mail, etc.

Style and colour

A small space needs a clean style and uncluttered look, though don't be afraid to use colour in moderation.

Potential and possibilities

Because this is a family home, which serves several different groups of people, it would be interesting to give visitors clues about the people who live here as soon as they enter the front door, which like the window, still has the original stained glass. The hall is structurally beautiful with high ceilings and, under a terrible carpet, a tiled floor. The hall is narrow but the long staircase with good banisters adds another plane to the room.

Design solutions

I took up the carpet to reveal the wooden stairs and magnificent tiled floor. I was then able to look at the room in terms of colour, texture and depth. I chose a strong blue for one wall to take the eye up the stairs

solution: panels add
subtle colour

solution: stone-coloured wall
reflects light

Add colour panels

Need to emphasize
the room's proportions
and bring in light

Unattractive old
carpet throughout

Before we started

After we finished

solution: blue wall extends up
stairwell to first landing

solution: original tiled floor
beneath carpet needed cleaning

Wall colours

Wall Colours

Using different colours of the same tonal value is the best way to add colour to a small space. The eye is not distracted or confused and the space is kept light.

and define the shape of the room. For the opposite wall I picked a stone colour to complement the floor and provide a neutral background for the panels.

Celia lent me her favourite book of plants and herbs and I used this as inspiration for the floor-to-ceiling panels, in which I echoed the fantastic colours of the facing stained-glass window.

The mosaic-framed mirror adds a modern twist to the hall. The key to its success is its size; if it had been any smaller it would have looked mean. As the room is narrow, I chose a console table to go against one wall, which provided space for the various items that needed a home, and the wastepaper bin, a must for all the junk mail, was given a makeover. The finished hall is a welcoming space that is not cluttered. The decorative scheme emphasizes the original features and yet remains fresh and contemporary.

Mosaic Mirror

This is one of my favourite projects in the book. It is stunning but so simple to make and, compared to shop-bought mirrors in the same style, amazingly inexpensive.

silvered tiles

Wastepaper Bin

There are endless ways to rejuvenate a bin, but I chose crackle glaze as it is tough, simple to use and striking.

skeleton leaves

Mosaic Mirror

Mirrors reflect light into dark corners, creating a sense of space and openness that the narrow entrance to this hall needed. Reinforce the effect by making a frame from silver leaf mosaic tiles to reflect even more light and dancing reflections. You can buy both mosaic tiles and finished mirrors in this style, but it is far cheaper to make your own.

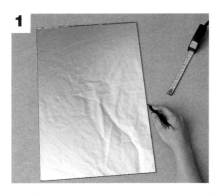

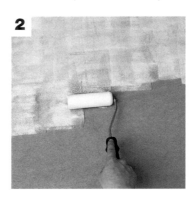

1. Place the mirror centrally on the MDF and draw round it.

2. Remove the mirror and prime the MDF with a solution of equal parts of PVA glue and water. It is best to use a sponge roller. Leave to dry then attach two keyhole fittings to the back of the MDF, so that you can hang the finished mirror. Glue the mirror to the centre of the MDF with mirror adhesive and leave it to dry overnight.

3. Paint the acrylic size onto the glass and leave it to become tacky. Lay sheets of silver transfer leaf on the glass, making sure that the edges butt up to each other. Fill in gaps with more leaf or, if it doesn't stick, apply more size and repeat the process. Brush off excess leaf with the soft brush. Decide on the size of the rectangle you want for the border by marking out two or three with masking tape on the glass. Get the rectangles cut by a glazier. It may seem wasteful to gild such a large piece of glass, but the silvering can get damaged in the cutting, so it is best to have some spare tiles.

4. To work out tile spacing before gluing, place them, leaf side down, a line at a time, around the mirror, working outwards.

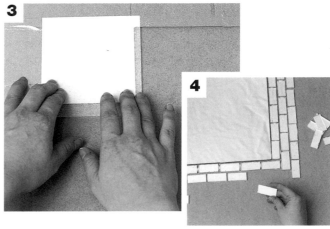

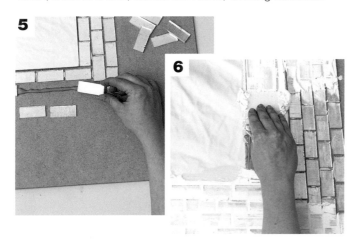

5. Working a small section at a time, remove some tiles, squeeze out a line of contact adhesive and place the tiles firmly onto it. Make sure that the tiles are evenly spaced and that the adhesive doesn't mark the tops of the tiles. Repeat the process with each line of tiles until you have reached the outside edge. Leave to dry overnight.

6. Working in sections, spread the grout over the tiles with a grout spreader, making sure that it fills all the gaps. Wipe the excess grout off with a damp cloth and then a dry cloth. Leave to dry overnight. You may have to repeat the grouting in areas, as the grout sometimes shrinks when it dries.

Mosaic Mirror

As an alternative to silvering your own tiles, you can ask a
glazier to cut mirror glass rectangles to the size you need.
These do work just as well, though the hand-silvered tiles
have a gentler quality that I think is worth the short time it
takes to make them. If silver doesn't work in your colour
scheme, try using tinted mirror glass and gold or copper leaf.

Wastepaper Bin

Revamp a wastepaper bin by creating a crackle effect in tans and browns. Add a touch of delicacy by gluing on a skeleton leaf. By using a traditional paint effect and adding an unusual detail, you can fuse the classical with the contemporary.

1. Paint the wastepaper bin with a base coat of tan-coloured acrylic paint and leave to dry.

2. Working on one section of the bin at a time, brush on the two layers of the crackle glaze.

3. Use a hairdryer to dry the glaze and produce some really defined cracks.

4. With your fingers, spread a fairly thin coat of burnt umber acrylic paint onto one section of the bin at a time.

5. Rub the paint well into the cracks with your fingers. Repeat the process on all the other sections of the bin and, when complete, leave it to dry.

6. Brush the leaves with a solution of equal parts of PVA and water. Place them in position and brush over them with more of the PVA solution.

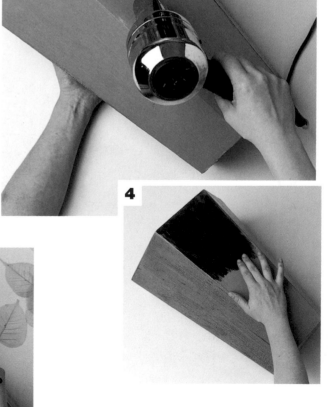

Wastepaper Bin

It is attention to the smallest details that really brings a decorating scheme for a room together, and this includes the bin. This project can be adapted to suit any colour scheme and design style. Paint the bin in a bold colour and rub a sharply clashing colour into the cracks for a vibrant look, or choose soft neutrals for a minimalist style.

Wall Panels

Make the most of high ceilings by making huge panels using stencils and spray paints. They are simple to make, but you do need a relatively large space, like a garden, to work on them.

shopping List

Motifs (see page 124)
Plastic stencil card
Masking tape
Hot stencil cutter
3mm- (¼ in-) thick MDF panel measuring 245 x 30cm (96 x 12in)
Stone-coloured matt emulsion paint
Layout paper or newspaper
Enamel spray paints in lime green and turquoise

1

2

1. Photocopy or draw out the motifs on page 124 to the required size. Lay plastic stencil card on top of each motif and secure it with masking tape. Cut out the main shape with the stencil cutter.

2. Paint the MDF panel with two coats of stone-coloured emulsion and leave it to dry. Tape the leaf stencil in place on the panel and cover any exposed areas around it with layout paper or newspaper. Spray lime green sparingly over the stencil, starting at the top. Gradually fade the colour by lifting the spray can further from the surface as you move up the stencil.

3. Gently peel the layout paper and stencil away. Leave to dry.

4. Cut another stencil for the veins on the leaves. Lay this stencil in place on the main shape and cover exposed areas as before. Spray the veins evenly with turquoise spray paint.

3

4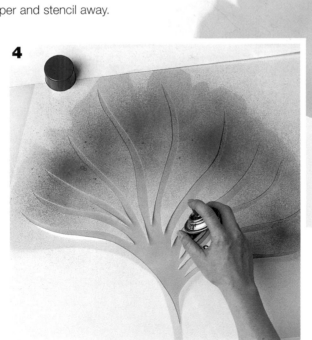

Wall Panels

You can make panels like these to fit any space and they are a brilliant, and decorative, way of covering up a damaged section of wall. The flower panel was made using the same methods as the leaf panel, just with different motifs. Choose themes personal to you and make up your own designs.

Woven Lampshade

Texture is the key here: the trick is to use natural fibres that have contrasting textures. By weaving hessian tape and soft chenille wool together you play with the contrast of the rough and the smooth.

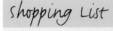

shopping List

Lampshade
Woven brown fabric tape
Scissors
Iron
Long, sharp needle
Sewing thread
Masking tape
Blue chenille wool
Darning needle

1

2

3
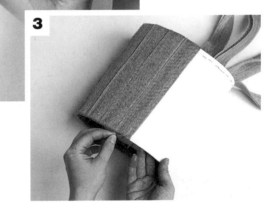

1. Measure the shade from top to bottom. Cut to this length, plus 5cm (2in), twice as many strips as you need to cover the shade. Fold each strip in half and press.

2 Sew each length of tape to the top of the shade with a long, sharp needle, using sewing thread and running stitch. Make sure that the edges of the tape are butted up tightly to one another.

3 Pull the lengths of tape taut down the lampshade and repeat the process around the bottom edge.

4 Trim the raw ends of the tape close to the stitching. Stick a length of cream-coloured masking tape over the raw ends to neaten them.

5 Thread the darning needle with a single strand of chenille wool and weave it in and out of the lengths of tape. Start at the top of the shade and work downwards, keeping the spacing between the rows of wool even.

4
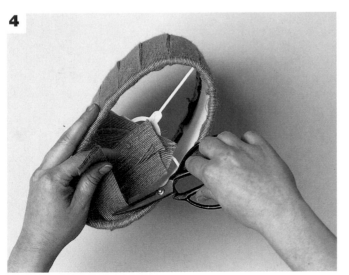

5

Woven Lampshade

The colours in this lampshade tone perfectly with the other colours used in the hall, helping to achieve a co-ordinated look. Remember that you must have an odd number of vertical strips to be able to weave the wool alternately over and under around the shade.

Decorating Solutions

Wall Flowers

To break up the strong vertical and horizontal planes of this room a little, I hung these arrangements of wildly twisting dried foliage on the wall. The holders are simply cut lengths of bamboo: if you cut them below a knot in the wood, the knot itself stops the plants falling through. I drilled a tiny hole in the back of each piece of bamboo and hung them from panel pins in the wall.

Letter Rack

One of the ongoing problems in most halls is correspondence. Post is often left lying around, and it just makes the room look messy. Solve this problem forever by staining a wooden letter rack to complement the colour of the wall behind it. Faithfully put all incoming or outgoing post into it and keep the area tidy.

Printed Paper

Printing from a leaf onto tracing paper is a stunning way to make your own writing paper. Always remember to make sure that the printed side is on the reverse. You can buy envelopes in the same paper, which can also be printed. Keep a supply, and some stamps and a pen, in your letter rack for dashing off answers to incoming post.

Console Tabletop

To personalize this console table we have laid some of Andrew's architectural drawings under a piece of glass cut to fit the tabletop. You can achieve a similar effect with almost anything, from your own sketches to copyright-free pen and ink drawings or your children's creations. It breaks up the tabletop and makes it more interesting.

Printed Plate

To hold all the bits and pieces that seem to end up in a hall, I have provided a shallow plate, which sits conveniently on the table. It has been mono-printed with a leaf design (see page 111 for basic instructions). However, instead of fabric paint, use satinwood paint to decorate the plate. Now all you have to do is empty the plate once a week and send the contents back to their proper homes.

Covered Address Book

Keep friend's addresses in a special address book. Either use a patterned fabric to cover the book, or print a design onto a pale, plain fabric. A tiny tassel adds a decorative touch. You can also cover diaries and business address books so that each is easily identifiable.

The Bedroom

New Way Ethnic

Sleep is important, but so is rest and reflection, the opportunity to just be alone with yourself. A bedroom should be more than just a place to rest one's weary head, it should offer an opportunity to indulge our dreams and comforts. The bedroom is the only place that is truly ours to do exactly what we want with. The temptation is to create a multi-functional and practical space, but this is not always comfortable or restful, so sometimes a bedroom should be just that, a bedroom.

This bedroom offers plenty of interest in terms of colour, depth and texture and yet is relaxing and peaceful at the same time.

Designer's Notebook

Wall colours

Whose room is this?

This bedroom belongs to Jessica, who is in her early twenties and is at university, but still lives at home with her parents during the holidays. As it is often unoccupied, the room has become a bit of a muddle of childhood and teenage fads and many of the furnishings have, quite frankly, seen better days.

What do they want from the room?

Jessica is close to her family and looks forward to the time she spends at home with them. She sees her bedroom as a place of peace where she can recharge herself after her busy life at university. She wants the room to inspire calm and enable her to indulge her femininity, but she definitely does not want frills. She wants the room to have longevity, in terms of being able to adapt it and maybe take the larger items with her when she eventually leaves home. She loves oriental fabrics and is keen to include as many as possible in the decorative scheme.

Colour and style

Jessica wants a gentle, feminine look in her room, but one that is contemporary and not fussy or cluttered.

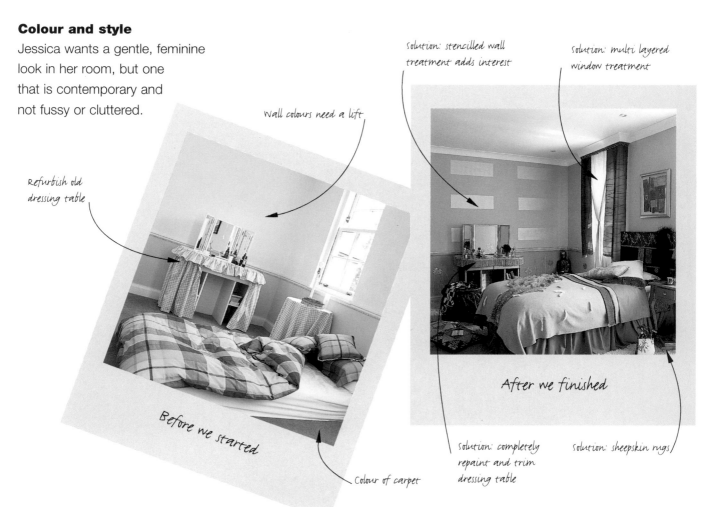

Wall colours need a lift

Refurbish old dressing table

solution: stencilled wall treatment adds interest

solution: multi layered window treatment

After we finished

Before we started

Colour of carpet

solution: completely repaint and trim dressing table

solution: sheepskin rugs

Copper transfer leaf stencil

Wall Treatment

Stencilling is a quick and effective way of transforming a large wall. The randomly spaced flowers prevent the pattern from looking too regular.

Metallic Finishes

Silver and copper reflect light and are a wonderful way of adding a subtle exotic element to a room, without going over the top.

Wall stencil colours

Possibilities and potential

As Jessica spends a lot of time away from home most of her possessions are at her university lodgings. So her room at home is quite bare and does not feel at all welcoming. It is a good size with simple detailing, but everything is rather flat with hard surfaces, it really needs some softness and texture.

The walls are a very strong colour, which Jessica has certainly grown tired of, and the dressing table is an old relic from her mother's past which has been dumped in her room. She rather resents it but it provides good storage and she cannot afford an alternative. Therefore she would like to make it over.

Design solutions

Jessica had to feel as though she had come home when she entered this room. She loved home and I needed to reflect that in the design. It also had to be a refuge for her and a place to relax and re-energize. Adding various softening influences was the

New Way Ethnic allows the spiritual elements of Eastern philosophies to filter through in colours and textures. At the same time it can accommodate modern day requirements and effervescent femininity. These are the words that I chose as my starting point.

Rest

Reflection

Home

Femininity

Fabric

Paint effects

Sewing

Silk painting

Crochet

Beads

Layering

Upholstery

Oriental

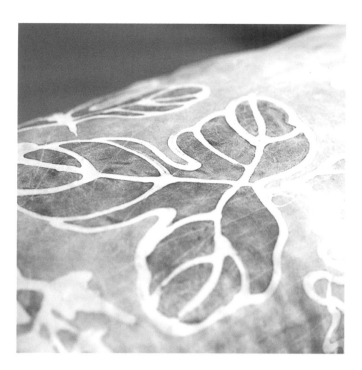

Painted Cushion Cover

Silk painting is both creative and relaxing, an ideal craft, in fact. I made this cover with a simple, tied-back opening, but you could add a zip or buttons if you wish.

Cushion fabrics

first step in getting this room to work. I divided the walls into two bands of colour. The top part was kept light and given a simple treatment with a soft sage-green background and large, bold rectangles of silver paint to break up the wide expanse of wall. The dividing dado rail was painted jade green and dragged to give a washed effect. The wall below the dado was painted a

darker shade of jade green, and then softened with stencilled silver reeds and gilded copper flowers.

I dressed the long, fairly narrow windows with a multi-layered treatment. Swathes of dyed muslin, gathered up with Indian bangles, hang behind satin window banners, which were stencilled in pink with the reed pattern used on the wall. To finish the windows off, a tiny feather 'pelmet' was attached to the cornice.

The dressing table was a bit of a challenge as it was all curtain and not much else. I had the basis of an

Dressing Table

several different materials went into this transformation, but none of them were costly.

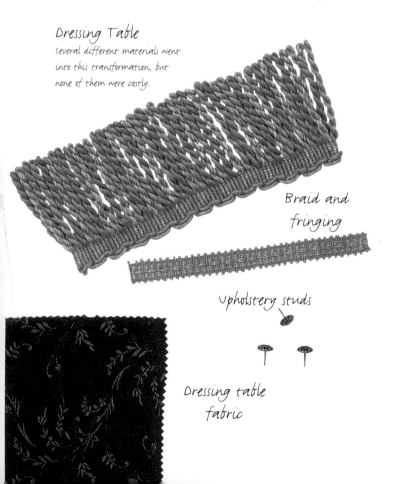

Braid and fringing

Upholstery studs

Dressing table fabric

Lampshade fabric and ribbon

Beads for lampshade

Ribbon and Beads
Inexpensive thin satin ribbon and tiny different-coloured beads are perfect for trimming fine fabric as they do not weigh it down.

Pleated Lampshade
Light from small lamps is so much more atmospheric, and flattering, than that from an overhead central light. Fine fabric diffuses the light even further.

interesting piece – a lovely kidney shape that was hiding under all that fabric. Oriental fabrics braid and fringing gave this old piece of furniture a new lease of life. The effect was well worth the effort and Jessica really loved her new dressing table. To diffuse the harsh lighting in the room, I pleated soft, silk organza around the existing lampshades and embellished them with sequins, ribbon and beads.

A base was bought for the bed (the only major expense) and I covered a headboard of MDF-backed foam with various printed fabrics. A soft woollen bedspread and freshly trimmed bed-linen, cushions bought on holiday in Greece, and another I made to suit the room, completed the transformation of the mattress on the floor. Little runners for the bedside table were made from the fabric used to trim the pillows.

Catkin Bedspread
Soft woollen fabrics and velvet or satin ribbons are physically and spiritually warming. There is nothing like wrapping up snugly in a blanket to make you feel cosy and content.

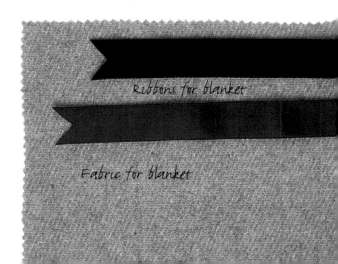

Ribbons for blanket

Fabric for blanket

Catkin Bedspread

In these days of duvets we have rather forgotten bedcovers, which is a shame as they can be so beautiful. Recycle a blanket or a length of wool fabric and cover it with crocheted catkins for a new look.

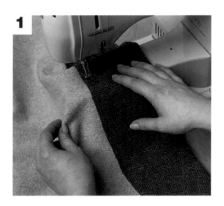

1. Wrong sides facing, fold the strip of contrast fabric in half widthways. Lay it over one end of the main fabric so that the end is against the fold in the contrast fabric. Machine the strip to the main fabric, taking a 1cm (¹/₂in) seam allowance and catching both sides of the strip in the line of machining.

2. Stitching close to the edge, machine ribbon over the raw edge of the contrast fabric. Machine along both edges.

3. Machine another length of ribbon to the other side of the bedcover in the same position. Stitch exactly over the lines of machining showing through from the first length of ribbon.

4. Crochet tubes, or 'catkins', of mohair wool (see page 122 for crochet instructions), each approximately 10cm (4in) long. For a double bedcover you will need about 40 catkins.

5. Lay the bedcover out flat and arrange the catkins, some

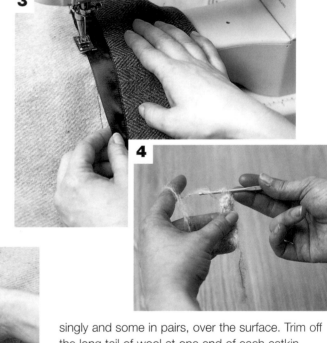

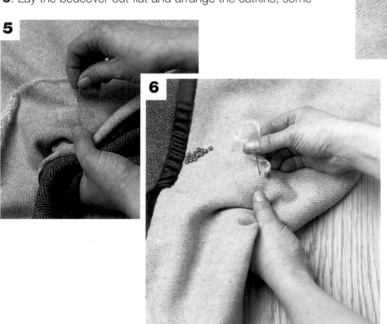

singly and some in pairs, over the surface. Trim off the long tail of wool at one end of each catkin. Thread a darning needle with the other tail and push it through the fabric where you want the catkin to be.

6. On the other side of the bedcover, take the needle through two glass beads then back up through the fabric. Take the needle through the bottom of the tube, back through the fabric, through the beads and up through the fabric again. Make a loop round the bottom of the tube, take the needle through the loop and pull the wool tight. Trim off the end.

Catkin Bedspread

If you don't want to crochet catkins, an alternative is to make them from felted wool. Cut a woollen sweater into strips and sew these into tubes. Boil-wash them in the machine to felt them and then attach them to the blanket as described in steps 5 and 6. This is a great way to recycle an much-loved sweater that is sadly way past its best.

Painted Cushion Cover

Painting your own fabric is extremely satisfying as you can be as modest or ambitious as you like. Create soft colours by adding water to your fabric paint and for a really dazzling effect, sprinkle rock salt onto the fabric whilst the paint is still wet.

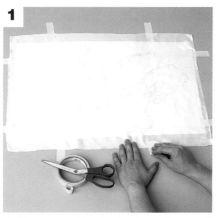

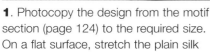

1. Photocopy the design from the motif section (page 124) to the required size. On a flat surface, stretch the plain silk over the design and secure it in place with masking tape.

2. Fill the dispenser with gutta and draw over the outline of the design. Leave to dry then slide the photocopy out from under the fabric.

3. When the gutta is dry you can begin to paint on the fabric paints. Mix them in jars according to the manufacturer's instructions. It's good fun to mix paints to create your own colours, so do experiment. First, cover the whole piece of silk with a flat colour and then build up your colours by filling the areas in between the gutta. Leave to dry and iron to fix the colours. Wash it gently with warm water and hand-washing detergent to remove the gutta. Leave to dry, then press.

shopping List

Cushion pad measuring 20 x 30cm (9 x 12in)

Motif (see page 124)

Piece of plain white silk measuring 23 x 33cm (10 x 13in) for the cover front

Masking tape

Gutta dispenser

Gutta

Fabric paints

Two pieces of dupion silk measuring 23 x 18cm (10 x 7in) for the cover back

Strips of dupion silk measuring 15 x 5cm (6 x 2in) for the ties

Pins

Sewing threads

Sewing machine

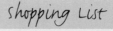

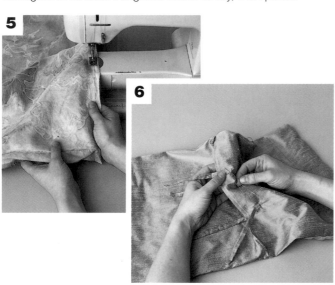

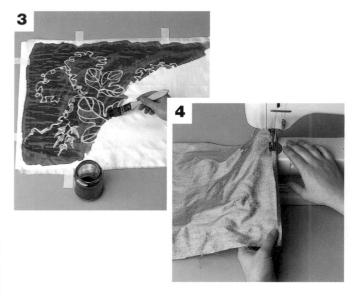

4. Make a 1cm (½in) double hem on one long side of each piece of dupion silk.

5. Wrong sides facing, lay the pieces of dupion silk onto the painted front with the hemmed edges overlapping in the middle. Tack then machine all round.

6. Fold the tie strips in half widthways then press the raw edges to the middle. Press under the short ends. Machine down the long side, close to the edge. Sew two ties to each side of the back cover opening.

Painted Cushion Cover

This is a traditional method of painting silk and has the advantage of using only cold ingredients. However, you can also use the hot wax batik method to make this style of cushion. For those of you who don't like to paint but do like to sew, the same motif could be appliquéd or embroidered, by hand or machine, onto a cushion cover.

Pleated Lampshade

This is an unashamedly feminine lampshade with soft fabric pleats and bead, sequin and ribbon trims. It is also a good way to breathe new life into an old shade, as long as it isn't strongly patterned or coloured.

shopping List

Lampshade

Two-tone chiffon, the length of the depth of the lampshade plus 10cm (4in), by three times the circumference

sewing thread

sewing machine

Fine, sharp needle

Iridescent sequins

Purple beads

Narrow ribbon

Gold beads

1. Machine a narrow double hem along both long edges of the chiffon.

2. Pleat the chiffon around the top of the lampshade in approximately 1cm (½in) pleats. Form one pleat at a time, butting each up to the previous one. Secure each pleat by bringing the needle and thread up through the centre of it, threading on a sequin then a purple bead, then taking the needle back down through the sequin and along to the next pleat. When you have pleated all round the shade, trim off any excess fabric and hand-stitch the short ends together.

3. Hand-stitch narrow ribbon around the bottom of the pleated fabric.

4. Stitch gold beads to the ribbon at regular intervals.

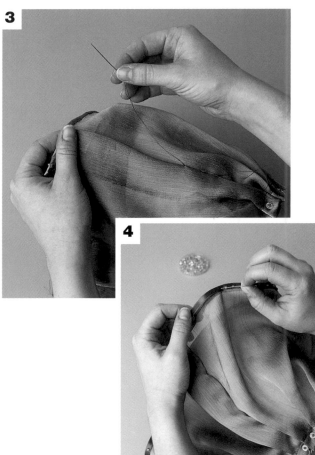

Dressing Table

Fabrics, trimmings and gilding turn an ugly dressing table into a sumptuous piece of furniture, which reflects the flavour of the room. Use woven, textured fabrics and colours with rich tonal values.

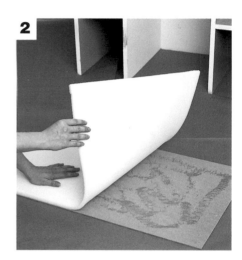

1. Paint the drawer fronts and the insides of the shelves with the satinwood paint and leave to dry.

2. Using the foam adhesive, glue a sheet of foam to one side of each of the outside MDF panels.

3. Working on one panel at a time, lay the panel, foam-side down, centrally on a piece of fabric. Fold the edge of the fabric to the back of the panel and staple it in place, gently pulling it taut so that it will be flat and smooth on the front. Repeat this process on the other panel.

4. Stick the panels to the outside of the dressing table legs with contact adhesive. It's a good idea to hold them in place with masking tape until the adhesive is dry.

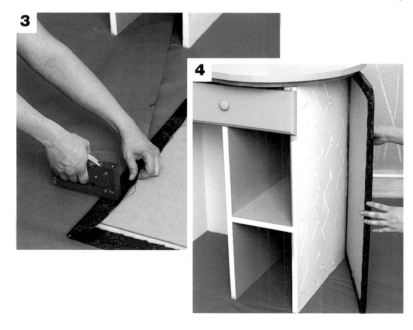

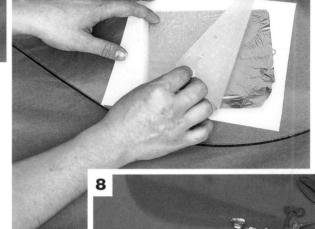

5. Make up the inside panels in the same way as the outside panels, but without the sheet of foam. Stick these panels in place and hold them with masking tape until the adhesive is dry.

6. Photocopy the flower motifs and arrange them under the glass. Fill in the outline with acrylic size, using a fine brush. Leave to become tacky to the touch; this should take about five to ten minutes.

7. Lay the copper transfer leaf over the motif and gently rub the paper backing with your fingers.

8. Gently peel away the paper backing and with small strokes, brush away the excess leaf with the soft brush.

9. Attach the bullion fringe to the edge of the dressing table top with decorative upholstery studs, hammering them in approximately 10cm (4in) apart.

10. Attach the flat braid to the fronts of the shelves in the same way as the bullion fringe.

11. Paint the frame of the mirror with the satinwood paint used for the shelves. When the paint is dry, add a little copper leaf to highlight the mouldings, using the technique explained in steps 6 to 8.

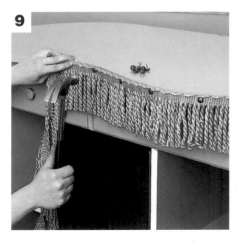

Dressing Table

To tie in with the newly refurbished dressing table I made a ruffled cover for an old stool. I used the same oriental fabric as I used for the outside panels of the table. The dressing table and stool now look like a set, rather than two separate, and once unwanted, items.

Wall Treatment

Using several different paint techniques and effects in soft greens and silver on the walls is interesting and gives a flavour of the East. Plan exactly where you want the rectangles to go before you start painting.

1

2

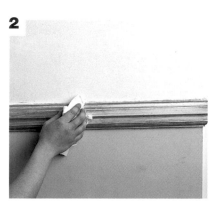

1. Paint the area below the dado rail with the darker green emulsion and leave it to dry. Dilute the dark green gloss paint to a watery consistency with white spirit and paint the dado rail with it.

2. While still wet, wipe over the gloss with a dry cloth, taking some of the paint off to create a washed effect. Leave to dry.

3. Paint the area above the dado rail with the lighter shade of green emulsion. Leave to dry.

4. Draw then cut out the reed motif from the stencil card with a craft knife. Tape the stencil card to one end of the wall, below the dado rail, with masking tape. Pour some silver acrylic paint into a roller tray, load the sponge roller with the paint and roller over the stencil.

5. Carefully peel off the stencil card. Re-tape the stencil to the wall a little further along, so that the motif continues seamlessly. Be careful not to smudge the first stencil. Repeat steps 4 and 5. Continue in this way until you have stencilled right round the wall.

3

4

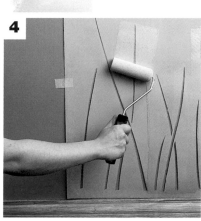

5

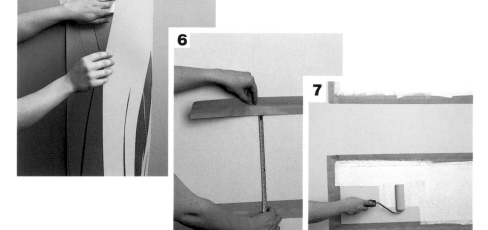

6

7

6. Above the dado rail, measure and tape out the rectangles. These can be as large or small as you want, but should all be the same size and repeat regularly across the wall. Use a spirit level to check that they are straight, as the shallowest slope will show.

7 With the sponge roller and silver acrylic paint, roller over the rectangles, being careful not to go over the tape onto the wall. Let the first coat dry and then roller on a second coat. Leave to dry and carefully peel off the tape.

Wall Treatment

Add gilded copper flowers, using the motif for the dressing table top (see page 126), to the stencilled reeds in key places to create a cohesive look. (See page 34 for gilding instructions.) If gilding does not appeal to you, stencil the flowers onto the wall with spray paint.

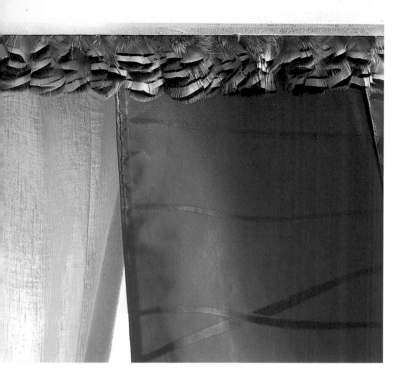

Decorating Solutions

Feather Pelmet

This is such a simple way to embellish a cornice, and to add an extra layer to a window treatment. These feathers can be bought in strips from good haberdashery shops, and you simply stick the top of the strip to the inside of the cornice.

Padded Headboard

The padded headboard was made in the same way as the outside panels for the dressing table (see page 83). The only difference is that it is larger and the foam is thicker. I sewed lengths of different fabrics together and then I stitched braid over the seams. I also printed a design onto the central panel of fabric using fabric paints, and sprayed it with fabric guard to protect it.

Table Runners

Miniature table runners, simply made from hemmed rectangles of oriental fabric, do a lot to dress up and soften a bedside table. You can print onto these or embellish them with ribbons or beads if you want to.

Bracelet Tiebacks

Children's Indian bracelets twinkle in the light, adding a touch of sparkle, and make very pretty alternatives to tiebacks. They are only really suitable for voile fabrics, however, as anything else will be too bulky to pass through them.

Printed Window Banners

For a window treatment that is a little different, print a bright contrasting colour onto a fairly dark, sumptuously coloured satin fabric, using the same stencil as for the wall treatment. This is yet another lovely way to bring the different elements in the room together.

Trimmed Bed-linen

This is such a simple way to get a really sophisticated, co-ordinated look in a bedroom. Simply turn under the raw edges of a strip of fabric and machine it around the open end of the pillowcase. I have used the same oriental fabric I used for the dressing table and table runners. If you use sheets, you can also sew a strip of the same fabric to the turndown.

The Bathroom

Faded Elegance

In these modern times, we take our bathrooms for granted: running water, showers, baths, privacy. We've forgotten how luxurious all this can be. There is something nostalgic about bathing, a word which suggests potions and aromatic oils, enjoyment in our cleansing ritual, preparing for the day ahead, getting ready for an occasion, or just simply having time to spend alone, soaking in a steaming bath. So move away from a stark, utilitarian look towards something softer and more atmospheric, then just enjoy it.

This bathroom is soft and inviting, full of warm colours which draw you in and attract your attention to the details. It is a place where you want to spend some time.

Wall colours

Designer's Notebook

Whose room is this?

This bathroom is in a small, modern, purpose-built apartment that belongs to Glen and Michelle. They both work but they do not have a lot of money to spend on decorating their home. The bathroom has a better than average bath, shower and sink, but it lacks character and it seems to be all practicalities with no style.

What do they want from the room?

Glen and Michelle want to get away from the ultra-modern look they have chosen for the rest of their apartment and create something softer and altogether more feminine and intimate. Storage is a major issue as Michelle loves toiletries but has nowhere to keep them. They both would like Michelle's personality to be reflected here, as after all, she does spend a great deal of her time in this room!

Style and colour

Gentle colours and luxurious fabrics are the key to softening a harsh bathroom.

Potential and possibilities

The bathroom has lovely tiles with a lilac tinge and gorgeous light coming in through the big window. The furnishings do not need replacing, but do need visually softening as the bathroom has quite a harsh feel.

Michelle has some lovely linen towels that she has collected over the years, but which have seen better days, and two purple frosted-glass vases, all of which she would like to keep.

Design solutions

I chose a colour scheme of dusky lavenders and lilacs, with shimmering antique gold and silver. I painted the walls in two complementary shades, then stencilled an intricate oriental chrysanthemum motif, in the same colours, onto the walls.

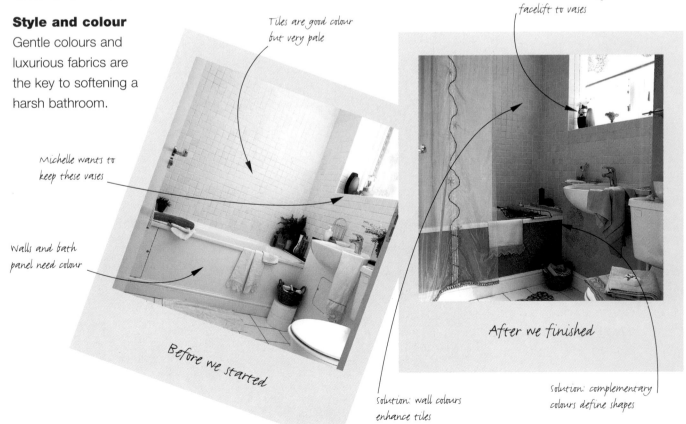

Tiles are good colour but very pale

Michelle wants to keep these vases

Walls and bath panel need colour

Before we started

solution: silver leaf gives facelift to vases

After we finished

solution: wall colours enhance tiles

solution: complementary colours define shapes

shower curtain trim

shower curtain fabric

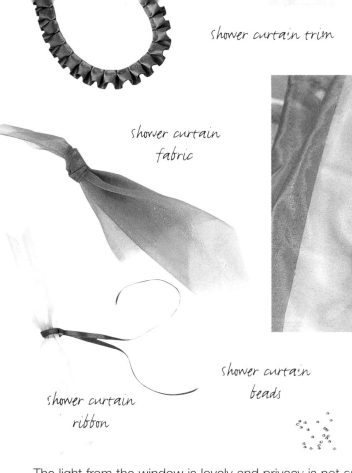

shower curtain beads

shower curtain ribbon

Faded Elegance captures all those things about the past that are about pure indulgence and attention to detail and yet it offers surprises. Choose colours that have a relaxing effect and make gentle, sophisticated use of materials and fabrics that play joyfully with the light; the appearance of which allows the mind to wander down memory lane. These words were my starting point.

Bathing

Embroidery

Frosting

Precious beads

Metallic thread

Silver

Gold

Sparkle

Stencilling

Bottles

Mosaic

Organza Shower Curtain
The ubiquitous plastic shower curtain is practical in every way, but hardly romantic or feminine. The answer is to cover it with another, more evocative, curtain. The plastic layer keeps the floor dry, while the fabric layer looks wonderful.

The light from the window is lovely and privacy is not an issue as the window is not overlooked, but both Glen and Michelle want to be able to control the amount of light. A blind is a good answer as it diffuses the light and is practical to operate. To tie the blind in with the rest of the room, I printed it with the chrysanthemum motif in a random pattern. Beaded fringing and a pull made from extra-special beads, which catch the light, make the blind a feature in its own right.

I really went to town with the shower curtain and chose metallic, antique-gold organza fabric. I appliquéd this with ribbon, stitched on with metallic thread, and embroidered it with gold flowers with bead stamens.

The splashtops in the bathroom are very stark, so I softened them with mosaic panels in shades that complement the walls.

A simple, and inexpensive, solution to storing Michelle's toiletries was to buy a number of identical bottles and frost them in interesting patterns. The much-loved linen towels were transformed from faded white to graduated lilac by dip-dyeing them and the vases were given a new lease of life with gilded patterns.

The end result is feminine without being overpowering, soft without being cluttered, and, which pleased Glen and Michelle, quite inexpensive to do and maintain.

Mosaic tiles

Details
Tiny elements, such as beads and mosaic, are really important in this design scheme.

Blind fringe

Organza Shower Curtain

Shower curtains don't have to be boring, go to town and make a truly desirable item so that every time you have a shower you feel like a movie star. Here, embroidery and beading are used to wonderful effect.

shopping List

Plastic shower curtain

Gold metallic organza fabric, the width of the shower curtain and the length plus 10cm (4in)

Organza ribbon

Gold metallic thread

Pins

Sharp embroidery needle

Satin ribbon

Gold bugle beads

Beading thread

Beading needle

Ribbon frill

Sewing thread

Metal eyelets

Hammer

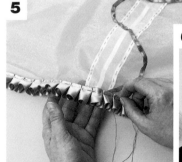

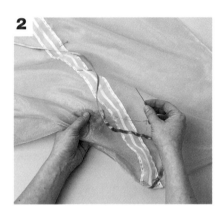

1. If the edges of the organza fabric are the selvedges, then simply leave them as they are. If they are raw edges, then machine a narrow double hem. With the gold thread and using running stitch, sew the organza ribbon to the organza fabric, about 20cm (10in) from the inner edge.

2. Next, sew on the satin ribbon in a wave, zigzagging across the organza ribbon. Use the gold metal thread again, but this time use a large chain stitch to hold the ribbon in place.

3. In alternate waves of the satin ribbon, and partly overlapping the organza ribbon, embroider a lazy-daisy-stitch flower in gold thread.

4. Make three stamens in the centre of each flower with gold bugle beads. Thread the beading needle with a length of beading thread and bring it up through the middle of the flower. Thread on 8 to 10 beads then, skipping the last bead, take the needle back down through the beads and into the fabric.

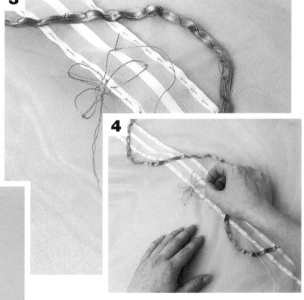

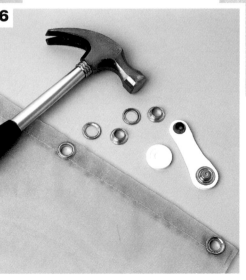

5. Sew the ribbon frill to the bottom of the curtain by hand.

6. Turn over and machine a double 5cm (2in) hem at the top of the curtain. Following the manufacturer's instructions, insert eyelets to correspond with those in the plastic shower curtain. Holding both curtains together, hang them from the shower rail.

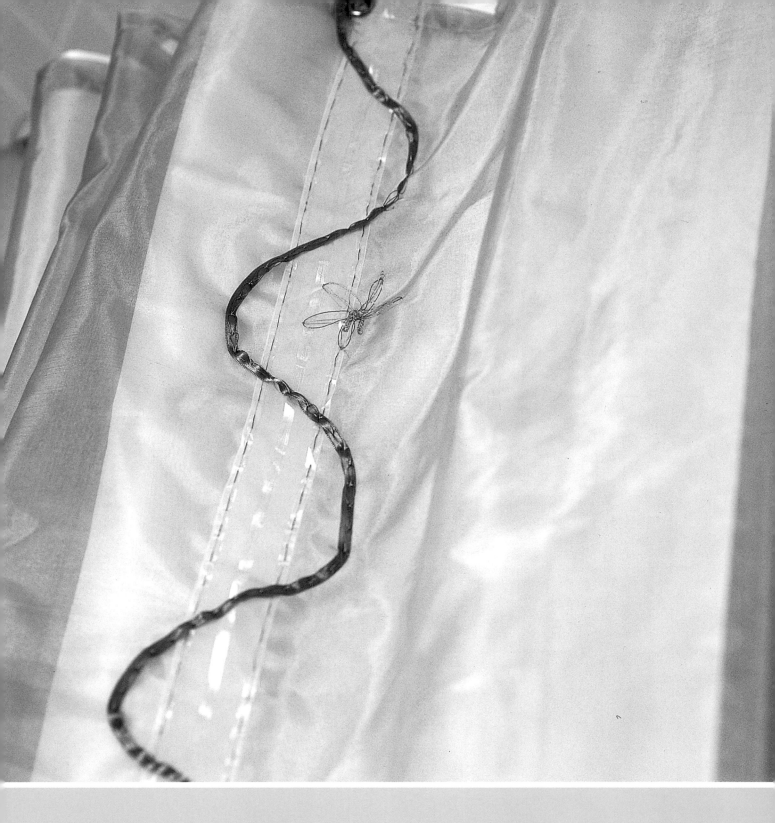

Organza Shower Curtain

You can let your imagination run wild with this project and
embellish the curtain as much as you wish. The secret lies in
co-ordinating the colours so that it doesn't look messy.
Remember, your embroidered shower curtain will need a
plastic one behind it to make it waterproof. Choose a white or
clear plastic one and it will barely show.

Frosted Bottles

There is something very desirable about frosted bottles. They soften their contents and offer a very classy way to store and display bubble bath, shampoo and oils. Frosting varnish is easy to use and can be adapted for use on glass bowls holding soaps and floating candles.

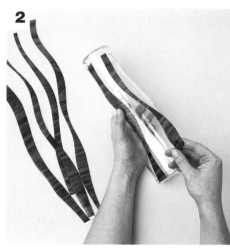

shopping List

sticky-backed plastic

Craft knife

Cutting mat

Plain glass bottles

Frosting varnish

Plate

sponge roller

1. It is a good idea to use a patterned or strong-coloured sticky-backed plastic as it makes it easier to see what you are doing. Cut simple shapes out of the sticky-backed plastic. I have chosen wavy stripes, and for another bottle, diminishing circles.

2. Place the sticky-backed plastic shapes on the bottle, ensuring that the edges are well stuck down.

3. Pour some of the frosting varnish onto a plate. With a clean sponge roller, roll the varnish evenly over the bottle.

4. Immediately peel the sticky-backed plastic carefully away to reveal clear glass patterns. You may find the craft knife useful for lifting the edge of the plastic. Allow the bottle to dry for at least half-an-hour before touching it further. It will, however, take a few days to dry completely, so be patient.

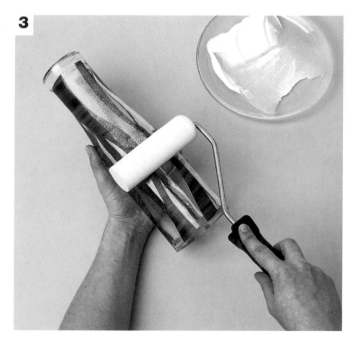

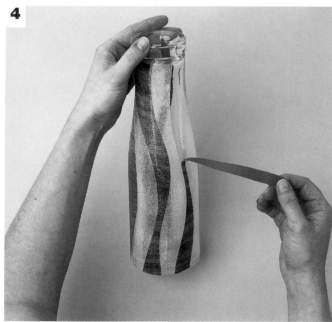

Frosted Bottles

Inexpensive plain glass bottles are given a new lease of life with frosted patterns. You can also add glass paint to the frosting varnish to tint it. If you know what colour oil you want to keep in the bottle, you could be really co-ordinated and frost the bottle in a colour to complement or contrast with the contents.

Mosaic Splash Panels

Softening and breaking up stark tiling can be achieved by making mosaic splash panels to complement your colour scheme. This design includes marble chippings, which are quick and easy to use.

shopping list

3mm- (⅛in-)thick MDF panels cut to size

Waterproof wood sealer

Paintbrush

Mosaic tiles in pink, lilac and purple

Tile snippers

Waterproof tile adhesive and grout combined

Grouting comb

Marble chippings

Contact adhesive

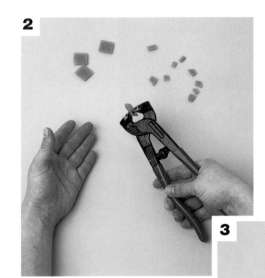

1. Seal both sides of the MDF panels with the waterproof sealer and allow to dry.

2. Cut the mosaic tiles into small pieces with the tile snippers.

3. Spread tile adhesive onto the panel with a grouting comb.

4. Place the mosaic tiles in wavy lines on the adhesive.

5. Place the marble chippings randomly between the mosaic lines. Leave the panel to dry then glue it in place with the contact adhesive.

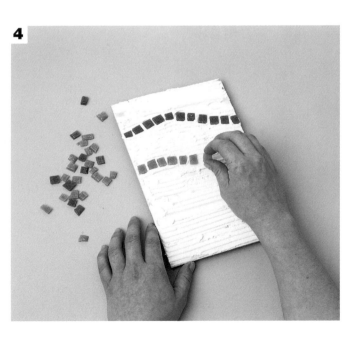

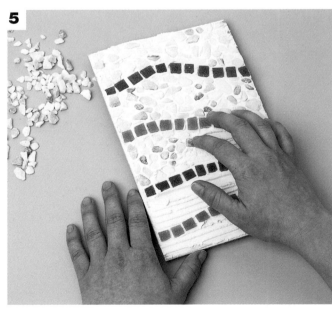

Mosaic Splash Panels

You can make variations of these panels by embedding glass nuggets, seashells, small smooth pebbles or coloured gravel (the kind sold for use in aquariums is ideal) into the grout. Remember that you have to be able to clean the panels, so avoid using anything that will tarnish or collect dust.

Dip-dyed Linen Towels

Dip-dye old linen towels to complement the colours and mood of your bathroom, and to give them a new lease of life. The graduated effect works well with pale colours like lilac, sky blue and dove grey.

shopping List

White linen towel
Metal or plastic basin
Plastic jug
Cold-water fabric dye
Water
Salt
Wire coat hanger

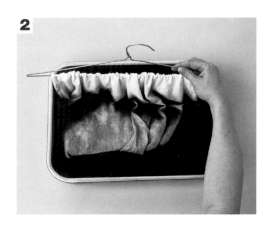

1. Mix the dye, water and salt according to the manufacturer's instructions. Use a basin large enough to hold the towel.
2. Fold the towel in half lengthways over the coat hanger. Dip the towel in the dye, making sure that all of it is submerged. Leave it in the dye for a few minutes.
3. Pull the towel out of the container and leave it to drip over the basin for another few minutes.
4. Repeat the process, each time dipping less and less of the towel into the basin, until you have achieved the depth of colour that you want. The whole procedure should take about 30 minutes. Wash the towel and leave it to dry.

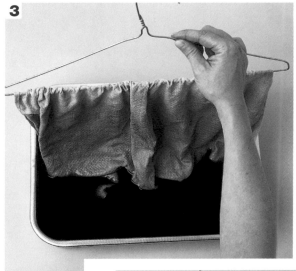

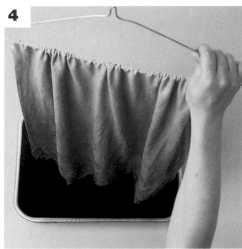

Stencilled Roller Blind

Stencilling an intricate chrysanthemum design is a simple and effective way of transforming an ordinary blind. On large windows it breaks up the expanse and comes to life when the light floods through.

shopping List

Plain cream-coloured roller blind
Chrysanthemum motif (see page 124)
Stencil card
Craft knife
Cutting mat
Fabric paint
Sponge roller
Plate

1. Enlarge the chrysanthemum motif on page 124 to the required size on a photocopier. Trace the motif onto stencil card and cut out the design with a craft knife on a cutting mat.

2. Place the stencil in position on the blind: I have stencilled the design randomly over the blind. Put some of the fabric paint onto a plate and with a clean sponge roller, roll paint over the stencil.

3. Peel the stencil carefully off the blind to reveal the image. Repeat the process until you are happy with the balance of the motifs on the blind. Allow the paint to dry before fitting the blind according to the manufacturer's instructions.

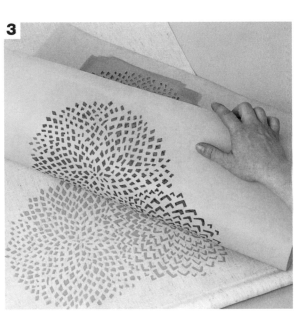

Decorating Solutions

Stencilled Walls

Continuing the chrysanthemum motif used on the blind onto the walls helps to unify the different surfaces in this small room. Stencil the motif onto the walls in exactly the same way as the blind, using a paint just a shade or two darker than the wall colour for a subtle effect. You could also experiment with pearlized paints, which shimmer and reflect light.

Gilded Vases

Gilding existing vases with silver transfer leaf in simple yet interesting patterns adds another touch of magic and sparkle. Choose a colour of transfer leaf to suit the vase and paint the designs straight onto the glass in acrylic size. (See page 34 for instructions for gilding onto glass.)

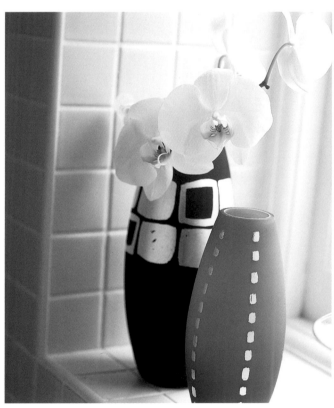

Creative Colour

To create subtle colour variations, without disturbing the newly acquired unity of the room, I painted the bath panel in the darker shade I used for the wall stencils. Then I continued the stencilled chrysanthemum motif, but in the lighter wall colour. Clever use of a limited paint palette in this way is both visually effective and easy on the pocket.

Blind Trimmings

A treasure for the bathroom in the most unexpected place: a beaded pull for the blind. To take full advantage of the light from the window, add a sparkling beaded trim to the edge of the blind. There are many different colours, lengths and styles of beaded trim available.

Dyed Towels

Machine-dye plain white towels to match your dip-dyed linen towels. Cotton towelling takes dye brilliantly and if the towels fade a little or get marked in time, simply pop them back in the machine with some more dye to refresh the colour.

Beaded Light Pull

Using the same principle as beaded blind trimming, create a light pull made from large glass beads: another exquisite detail to delight the eye. Mix gold and silver beads with the odd Venetian glass bead to make it extra-special. String them onto nylon-coated tension thread, which is strong and will stand the test of time.

The Garden

Functional Feng Shui

The garden often gets ignored when it comes to design ideas. It can require hours of weeding, mowing and watering, and is, therefore, sometimes very beautiful but not very relaxing or much fun.

Small gardens or outside spaces are precious but are often not used to their full potential. So, think of the outside, if you will, as sanctuary, a place to recharge your batteries and enjoy colours, smells, sounds and the feel of the air. Plant scented flowers and use vibrant colours to stimulate the senses and refresh the mind.

Create an outside space that feels like a room with no ceiling. The smallest garden can be given a sense of space with careful planning and design.

Designer's Notebook

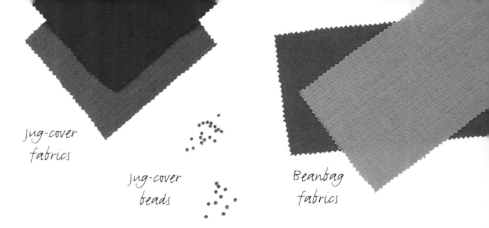

Jug-cover fabrics

Jug-cover beads

Beanbag fabrics

Whose garden is this?

Brian and Lucinda are both successful photographers, who lead busy professional lives and equally busy social lives. They love entertaining in their garden but there never seems to be enough room and there is nowhere for everyone to sit.

What do they want from the garden?

When life is a little quieter, they love to sit in the garden and just spend time together, reading, chatting or simply enjoying the colours and smells around them. Their home is full of colour and interesting things collected over the years and they would like their garden to be an extension of this, almost another room.

They have storage space in the shed, so they can store some things but they can't be too bulky and should ideally fold up or pack flat.

Possibilities and potential

Although the space is small, it has lots of potential for interesting nooks and crannies to suit different moods, but which can also work as a whole. Because they lead such busy lives, as do most of their friends, I wanted to create a calming environment with colours that are uplifting and that lighten the heart. I chose strong acidic colours, to remind them of sun and summer all year round. I suggested mandarin oranges, bright saffron yellows, turquoise blue and splashes of fuschia pink.

Design solutions

The plants are mature and make the garden feel established and grounded, so I decided to leave those alone. However, I wanted to break up the space so that it would work for different activities, as well as moods.

Style and colour

Brian and Lucinda love the sun and want a look that will remind them of it, no matter what the weather.

Bench needs attention

Add interest to shed

Before we started

space needs definition and division

solution: blue cactus cupboard breaks up white shed

solution: bench is re-coloured and has new cushion pad

After we finished

solution: screen adds flowing curves

solution: different tables help to divide space

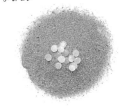

Pebble Candles
You can make your own candles in almost any shape you want. They provide the most lovely light and they are great fun to make.

Candle wax and sand

Pebble

Zen Table
Real wood is quite expensive, but this table requires only a minimum, and the effect is well worth the money.

Ash wood

I started by building two tables on the same principle, but at different levels, one for eating at and one as an occasional table. The shallow sand-pit in the centre can be made purely decorative by covering it with glass, or it can be left open and used as a mini Zen garden.

Lucinda and Brian wanted to keep the bench so I decided to do a makeover with a teak wood treatment. To make it more comfortable I added a quilted seat pad. I provided extra seating with beanbags, which are fun and practical and can be stored in the shed. I used hard-wearing, washable fabrics in orange and yellow. Funky, moulded chairs continued the colour statement and could also be stacked in the shed.

A water feature made from a sand-coloured, concrete bowl with a gentle pump, filled with pebbles and surrounded by a bamboo screen and plants, created a gentle, reflective mood as you entered the garden and immediately set a calm scene.

Eating and drinking outdoors is always a pleasure tempered by insects, and although jug covers do suggest a particular era, I believe they are invaluable for outside catering. I made my own versions from coloured fabrics with different beading techniques. Another similar idea is to stud a wire food cover with daisies to make it pretty as well as practical.

This small garden has been completely transformed into a tiny oasis of colour and tranquillity, the perfect spot for sunny Sundays and convivial evenings.

Themes

Functional Feng Shui fulfils all I think that design for the garden is about. It requires you to look at the natural elements and then incorporate them into your scheme. I jotted down these words to inspire me.

Outside

Entertaining

Friends

Sand

Candles

Beading

Wood

Sanctuary

Organic

Function

Printing

Colour

Light

Zen Table

Zen gardens are truly wonderful and you can make your own version in any size or shape you want. Protect the patterns under glass or leave the sand exposed with a comb next to it; no-one will be able to resist the temptation to make their own patterns. Alternatively, nestle pebbles and flowers into the sand, alongside tempting refreshments.

shopping List

18mm- (³/₄in-) thick MDF base the size you want the table to be

Four 30 x 2.5cm (12 x 1in) ash planks, each the length of one side of the MDF base minus 30cm (12in)

Panel pins, shorter than the thickness of the planks

Hammer

Four 3cm- (1¼in-) wide veneer strips, each the length of a side of the MDF base.

Iron

Cloth

Varnish

Fine sand

Wide-toothed comb

Glass

1. Place one ash plank under one side of the MDF, aligning the corners. Hammer in panel pins all the way along the outer and inner edges, approximately 10cm (4in) apart. Make sure you use the correct length pins as they must not break through the ash on the right side.

2. Butt the short end of a second plank up to the long edge of the first. The outer corner of the second plank and the second corner of the MDF should align. Use panel pins as before to hold the plank in place. One at a time, place the remaining two planks in the same way and hold them in position with panel pins.

3. Working on one side of the table at a time, lay a veneer strip against the edge. Place a cloth over it and use a hot iron and firm pressure to melt the glue. Apply two coats of varnish to the whole table.

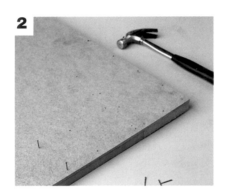

4. Pour the fine sand into the well in the centre of the table top.

5. Use a wide-toothed comb to level the sand and to make patterns.

6. Add extra patterns with your fingers. When you are happy with the design, you can place a sheet of glass over the table to protect it.

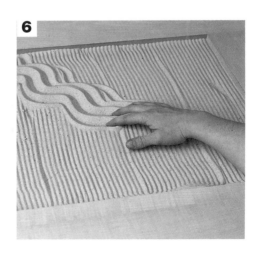

Zen Table

As well as being decorative, this table is immensely practical.
A table-top barbecue can be firmly planted in the sand, and
plates and glasses nestled alongside. If the sand gets dirty,
simply replace it.

Jug Covers

You may think that covers like these are old-fashioned, but when the wasps and flies smell your delicious drinks and zoom in, these covers come to the rescue. As they are simple to make and pretty to look at, you can use left-over scraps of fabrics from other projects and sew a cover for each of your jugs.

Shopping List

Fabric

Plate

Tailor's chalk

Scissors

Pins

Sewing thread and needle

Beading thread and needle

Beads

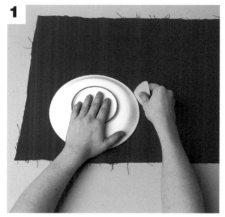

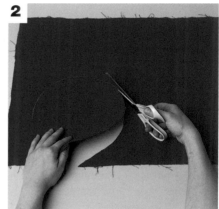

1. Place the plate on the fabric and draw round it with tailor's chalk.

2. Cut out the circle.

3. Turn over a narrow double hem and stitch it down by hand with hemming stitch.

4. With beading thread and a fine beading needle, take a stitch in the fabric then thread sixteen beads of the same size onto your needle, followed by a larger bead and then one the same size as the original sixteen. Missing the last bead, take

the needle back through the beads and secure the thread by oversewing the edge of the fabric. Repeat the process, stitching on lengths of beads about 5cm (2in) apart, until you have completed the circle.

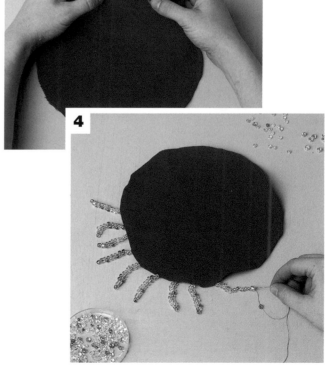

Bench Cushion

A bench seat outside is lovely to sit on side-by-side and chat, but for those really in-depth conversations, a comfortable seat pad makes all the difference. Again, use bright colours that encourage uplifting thoughts and glow in the sunlight.

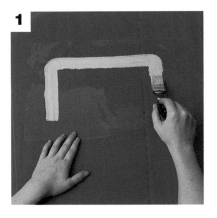 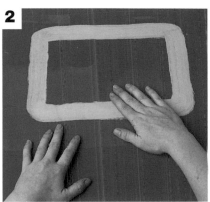

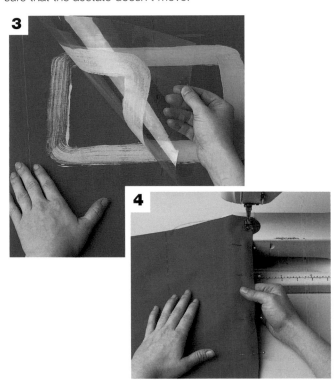

shopping List

A piece of padding the size of the bench seat

Fabric paint

2.5cm (1in) household paintbrush

Acetate

Iron

Two pieces of sheeting, each 5cm (2in) larger all round than the bench seat

Pins

sewing machine

sewing thread to match fabric

sewing needle

Four strips of sheeting 20cm (8in) long by 8cm (3in) wide

1. Test the fabric paint on a spare piece of the fabric first to check the colour density. If it disappears into the fabric, you can add white paint to make the colour more opaque. Lay one piece of fabric on a flat surface that is protected with plastic or paper. Paint rectangles onto the acetate: it doesn't matter if they aren't perfect. If you're not pleased with a shape then just wipe it off and start again.

2. When you're happy with the rectangle, place the acetate paint-side-down on the fabric and rub the back firmly, making sure that the acetate doesn't move.

3. Gently peel off the acetate. If the painted rectangle doesn't seem strong enough, repeat the process, making sure that you overlap the edges of the original rectangle. Print smaller or larger squares and rectangles randomly all over the fabric. Leave to dry then lay the printed side of the fabric on a clean, old cloth and iron it on the back. Leave the second piece of sheeting plain.

4. Right sides facing, pin the two pieces of sheeting together. Machine round three edges, creating a bag with one short edge open.

5

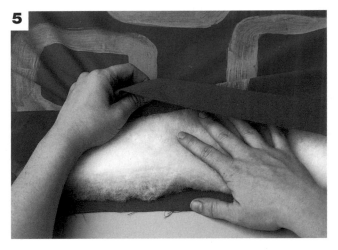

6

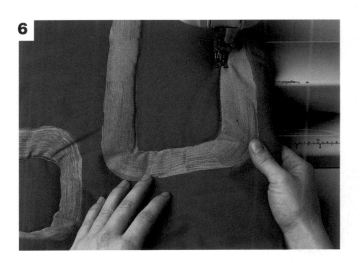

7

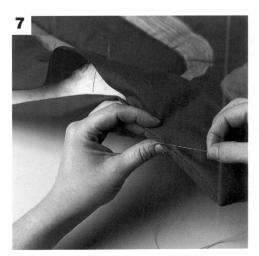

5. Slide the padding into the bag and make sure that it lies flat and reaches each corner.

6. Quilt the pad by machining around the inner edge of each painted rectangle, through all the layers. If the layers slip, use pins to hold them in place before machining.

7. Trim away any excess padding and hand-stitch the opening closed.

8. Fold the four strips of sheeting in half lengthways then press the long raw edges to the middle. Press under the short raw edges. Topstitch close to the open edge to make ties.

9. Hand-stitch two ties to each of the back corners of the cushion and use them to tie the cushion to the bench.

8

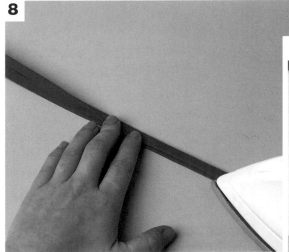

9

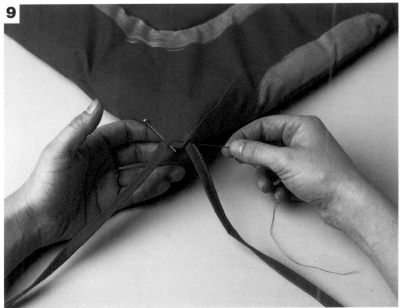

Bench Cushion

This bench was structurally sound but looking rather worse for wear after several years in the sun and the rain. To make the wood as smart as the new cover, I sanded it all down to remove any old varnish, then stained it with a teak-coloured waterproof wood stain. A couple of coats of varnish sealed it and prepared it for more summers and winters to come.

Pebble Candles

As night falls in your outside space, light up pebble-shaped candles. A good way to keep insects at bay is to add a few drops of citronella essence to the candle mix before you pour it into the moulds.

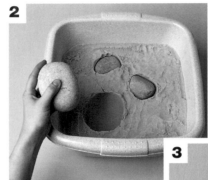

1. Half fill the washing-up bowl with damp sand and push the pebbles into it. Push each pebble in about halfway.

2. Carefully lift the pebbles out to reveal the mould shapes.

3. Measure out the stearin and wax colour according to the manufacturer's instructions. Put the stearin in a double-boiler and melt it over a gentle heat. The stearin allows the wax colour to disperse easily.

4. Add the wax colour to the liquid stearin and melt it over a gentle heat.

5. Measure out the paraffin wax into the pan and melt it over a gentle heat, still using the double-boiler and stirring occasionally.

6. When the wax mixture has completely melted, very carefully pour it into the moulds. Make sure that no sand falls into the mixture. Leave to set for one hour

7. With a skewer or wick needle, make a hole in the centre of each candle and push the wick in. Top up the wax if necessary and leave for at least 5 hours to set. Before you light the candles, trim the wicks.

Pebble Candles

You can use the same method to make candles to almost any shape and size. The candles by the bath on pages 90-91 were made by forming the mould in the sand with the end of a piece of wood. (See page 14 for basic instructions for this style of mould making.) Fill the moulds with layers of different coloured waxes for an interesting striped effect.

Beanbag Covers

Beanbags are always fun and are great for the garden as they are easy to move and store. Make removable and washable covers from hardy fabric in strong colours to evoke bright, heady summer days.

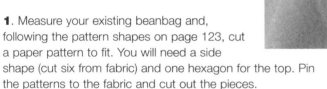

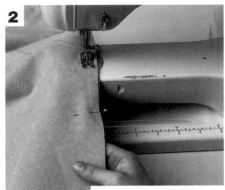

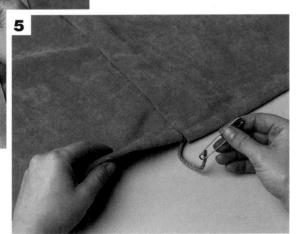

1. Measure your existing beanbag and, following the pattern shapes on page 123, cut a paper pattern to fit. You will need a side shape (cut six from fabric) and one hexagon for the top. Pin the patterns to the fabric and cut out the pieces.

2. Right sides facing, pin the side pieces together and machine, taking a 1.5cm ($^5/_8$in) seam allowance. Machine from the small end to about 4cm (1$^1/_2$in) from the large end of each side piece.

3. Turn under the raw, unsewn sides leading to each large end. Then, turn over a 1cm ($^1/_2$in) then a 2cm ($^3/_4$in) hem across each large end. Machine close to the folded edge. The

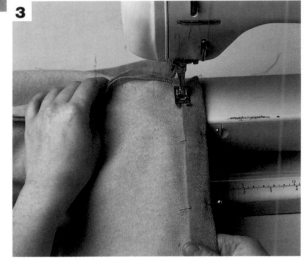

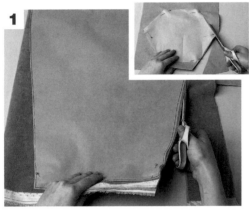

hem must be wide enough for the cord to pass through.

4. Pin the hexagon to the raw small end of each side piece and machine all round.

5. Attach a safety pin to one end of the cord and thread it through the channels in the large ends. Put the cover over your existing beanbag, pull the cord up tight and tie it in a double knot.

Beanbag Covers

Making washable covers means that you don't have to worry about the beanbags getting dirty, which they will undoubtedly do in a garden. If you are a keen needleworker you could consider appliquéing motifs onto the covers to complement other items you have made for the garden, such as jug covers or a bench cushion.

Pebble Water Fountain

There's nothing quite like the sound of running water to soothe the mind. This fountain is very much in the spirit of feng shui and uses natural elements that are represented in this outside space.

shopping List

Cement bowl with hole drilled three-quarters of the way up the side

Pump

Wire mesh

Marker pen

Wire cutters

Pebbles

Water

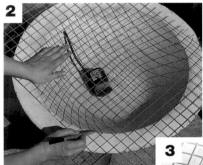

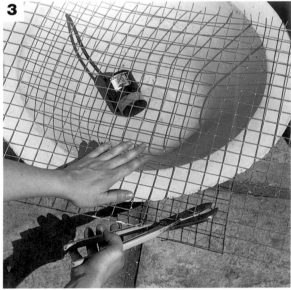

Ask the supplier to drill the hole in the cement bowl for you or, alternatively, you can do it yourself with a masonry drill bit. Read the instructions on the pump you buy carefully and if necessary, adapt the following steps to suit it.

1. Put the pump in the centre of the bowl and push the power cable through the hole. Attach the plug.
2. Lay the wire mesh over the bowl and draw onto it, following the line of the inner rim.
3. Cut along the drawn line with the wire cutters. Push the mesh into the bowl, making sure that it sits above the drilled hole and that the pump head is poking through the mesh.

4. Arrange the pebbles on the wire until it is completely disguised and all you can see is the pump head.
5. Pour water into the bowl then plug in and switch on the pump.

Pebble Water Fountain

Surround your fountain with plants to create a little oasis in a patio garden. If you prefer, you can cover the wire netting with seashells, but you will need a lot of large shells to do this. If you decide to use shells, please make sure that they come from a reputable supplier. Damage to the seabed by some methods of shell collecting is a major environmental concern.

Decorating Solutions

Lanterns

As well as candles, here is another lighting solution for your evening garden. One or several lanterns can make all the difference between talking to your friends, or mistaking them for the rose bush. The beauty of these lanterns is that you can move them around to create pools of light, and you can take them on picnics. Use citronella candles to keep insects away.

Bamboo Screen

A flexible bamboo screen is a great way to change the shape of your outdoor space. You can use it in front of flat walls to create soft curves and to hide ugly bricks. Alternatively, screen off areas and create a special, private corner where you can sit and read, or just enjoy the sun. Screens can be bought from good garden centres, or if you are feeling ambitious, you can make your own from lengths of bamboo tied together with wire.

Cactus House

A simple mini-greenhouse painted in a blazing Mediterranean blue, filled with miniature cacti or succulents is both easy to look at and easy to maintain. Attach it to a blank bit of wall in your garden, which, for the best effect, should be white.

Wind Chimes

A wind chime not only looks lovely swaying in the breeze, but it also has a restful effect on the ears, as long as the wind doesn't blow too hard. Hang one in the branches of a tree for maximum effect.

Flowered Food Covers

To complement your jug covers (see page 110) and protect your food from insects, use old-fashioned food covers. These are commercially available and really are very useful. However, they aren't particularly pretty. Overcome this by pushing flower heads into the wire mesh to create a combined food cover, flower display for your table.

Ice Sculptures

Instant art, which cools you down by just looking at it. Fill a cylinder or conical mould with water and keep it in the freezer. At a moment's notice you can create an interesting feature: simply sprinkle petals all over it and enjoy.

Patterns and Instructions

Pattern for Knitted Throw (see page 54)

Materials
Rowan chenille yarn
Pair of 5mm (No. 6/US 8) knitting needles

Abbreviations
k – knit
mb – make bobble. Knit into front and back of stitch twice.
Turn, p 4. Turn, k4. Turn, p4. Turn, k4. Pass 2nd, 3rd, and 4th
sts over 1st st.
p – purl
ss – stocking stitch (1 row k, 1 row p)
st/s – stitch/es

For each bobble square:
Loosely cast on 41 sts.
Rows 1-4 ss, starting with k row.
Row 5 k 15, mb, k to end.
Rows 6-12 ss.

Row 13 k 31, mb, k to end.
Rows 14-24 ss.
Row 25 k 6, mb, k to end.
Rows 26-30 ss.
Row 31 k 30, mb, k to end.
Rows 32-36 ss.
Row 37 k 34, mb, k to end.
Rows 38-46 ss.
Row 47 k 10, mb, k to end.
Rows 48-54 ss.
Row 55 k 24, mb, k to end.
Rows 56-59 ss.
Row 60 cast off in k.

For each plain square:
Loosely cast on 39 sts.
Work 59 rows in ss, starting with a k row.
Row 60 Cast off in k.

Beading instructions for Beaded Table Mats (see page 36)

Thread a beading needle with beading thread and double it. Thread a bead over the needle and, close to the end of the thread, tie a firm double knot around the bead, which is number 1 on the diagram below. Thread on ten more beads, then take the needle back through bead number nine. Thread on another bead, number 12, then take the needle through bead number seven. Pull the thread up quite firmly and you will see that the beads start to form two rows. Continue adding beads, taking the needle through each odd-numbered bead of the first row, working up to the top of the row. Then tread on another bead and start to work back down the row again.

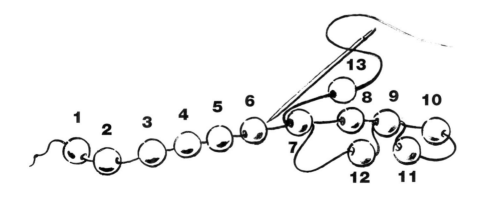

Crochet instructions for Catkin Bedspread (see page 78)

Materials

Mohair wool in two colours
Size 5 crochet hook

1 Make loop in one end of a ball of yarn. Push the crochet hook through the loop, take the wool over it and pull the hook back through the loop to make a stitch.
2 Repeat the process and make five more stitches.
3 To make a circle, push the hook through the first stitch, take the wool over it and pull the hook back through the same part of the stitch.
4 You now have two stitches on the hook. Take the wool over the hook and pull the hook through both stitches to make one stitch, so completing the first row of stitches.
5 To start the second row push the hook through the top of the second stitch, take the wool over the hook and pull the hook back through the same part of the stitch. Continue to work in the same way, going round and round in a spiral to make a crocheted tube. The tube should naturally tighten as you work up it, but if it doesn't then when it is about 5cm (2in) long, skip the occasional stitch. Crochet the tubes until they are about 10cm (4in) long. To cast off, cut the yarn approximately 15cm (6in) from the hook and take the cut end through the last stitch and pull it up tightly.

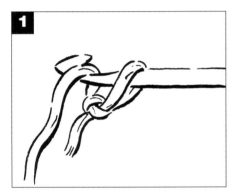

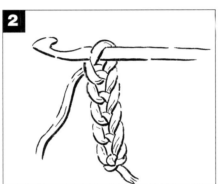

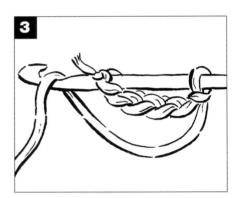

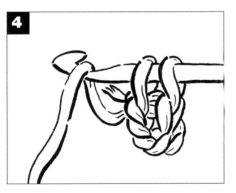

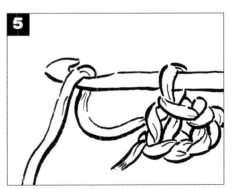

Pattern pieces for Beanbag Covers (see page 116)

Cut six side pieces (left) and one top piece (right) for each beanbag cover

Arrow shows direction of fabric grain

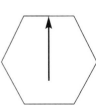

Motifs

You can use the templates on these pages as motifs for gilding, stencilling or painting. To make a stencil, enlarge the template to the required size on a photocopier then tape the photocopy to a window with low-tack masking tape.

Tape the stencil card over the photocopy. The light coming through the window will allow you to see through the stencil card to the photocopied template. Trace off the template onto the card and then cut out the stencil with a craft knife on a cutting mat.

Leaf motifs for Appliqué Cushions (see page 30)

Fish and seaweed motifs for Gilded Table Runner (see page 34)

Leaf, leaf vein and flower motifs for Wall Panels (see page 66)

Motif for Painted Cushion
Cover (see page 80)

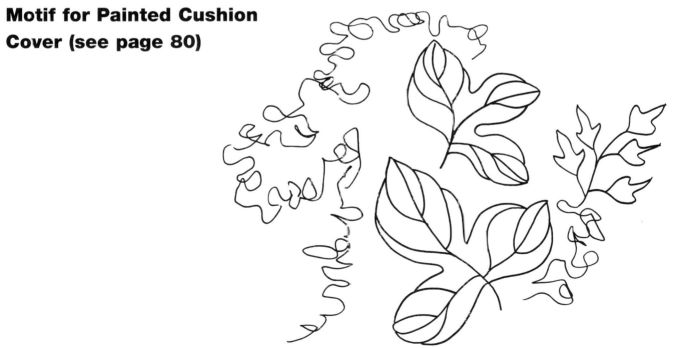

Flower motifs for Dressing Table (see page 83)

Reed motifs for Wall Treatment (see page 86)

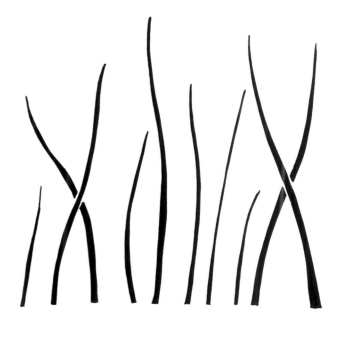

Chrysanthemum motifs for Stencilled Roller Blind (see page 101)

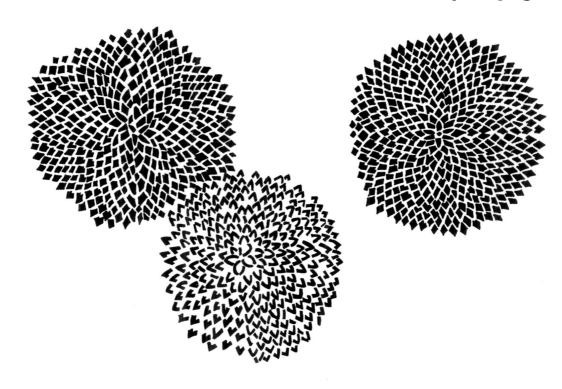

Suppliers

Andrea Maflin Partnership
Unit 3, 42 Orchard Road, Highgate,
London N6 5TR
Tel: 020-8348 6828
Fax: 020-8348 5909
E-mail: design@andreamaflin.co.uk
Website: www.andreamaflin.co.uk
Innovative bespoke decorative services

B & Q Plc *Head Office*, Portswood
House, 1 Hampshire Corporate Park,
Chandlersford, Hampshire, SO53 3YX
Tel: 01703-256256
Paint, wood, panel pins, screws,
mirror screws, sandpaper, silver sand
and sand plus general DIY materials

Barnett Lawson Trimmings Ltd
Little Portland Street, London, W1
Tel: 020-7636 8591
Fax: 020-7580 0669
Trimmings, ribbons, tapes, feathers

Bolloms Display *Head Office*,
PO Box 78, Croydon Road,
Beckenham, Kent, BR3 4BL
Tel: 020-8658 2299
Fax: 020-8658 8672
Suedette, PVC, felt

Bond & White Buildbase
40 Muswell Hill Road, London, N6
Tel: 020-8883 9722
Fax: 020-8444 5146
General DIY

Borovicks 16 Berwick Street,
London, W1V 4HP
Tel: 020-7437 2180/0520
Fax: 020-7437 2180
Fabrics of all descriptions, including
suedette, oriental, voile, dupion silk,
wool, velvet

Candlemakers Suppliers
28 Blythe Road, Olympia,
London, W4 0HA
Tel: 020-7602 4031
Fax: 020-7602 2796
Candle-making materials,
gutta, fabric dyes

Design Warehouse Ltd
Kingfisher House, Copse Lane,
Hayling Island, Hants, PO11 0BQ
Tel: 01705-466066
Fax: 01705-466262
Artech Angled Tip Stencil Cutter,
stencil paint

Dylon International Ltd
Home Dye Mfrs, Worsley Bridge
Road, London, SE26
Tel: 020-8663 4801
Cold-water, machine-, hot-water
and batik dyes

Edgar Udny & Co
314 Balham High Road,
London, SW17 7AA
Tel: 020-8767 8131
Mosaic tiles, tile cutters

Ells & Farrier, 20 Beak Street,
London, W1R 3HA
Tel: 020-7629 9964
Mail order, Denmark Works,
Beamond End, Amersham, HP7
0RX
Tel: 01494-715606
Fax: 01494-718510
Beads, findings, beading supplies

Fantasy Fayre
22 Camden Road,
London, NW1 9TD
Tel: 020-7916 2100
Haberdashery

Goodwoods 106 Junction Road,
London, N19
Tel: 020-7272 6569
Fax: 020-7561 9549
Wood, MDF, veneers

John Lewis Partnership
call 020-7629 7711 for branches
Fabric, curtain tapes, scissors,
threads, dyes, trimmings, ribbons,
embroidery threads, needles, pins
knitting needles, wool

Leyland Paints *Head Office*,
45 Farringdon Road, London EC1
Tel: 020-7405 8985
Stapleguns, sandpaper, paints,
paintbrushes, crackle glaze spray
paints

London Graphic Centre
Unit 9–10 Mckay Trading Estate,
Kensal Road, London, W10 5BN
Tel: 020-7739 7766
Spray paint, fabric paint

Marchmade 79 Dean Street,
London, W1 6HY
Tel: 020-7437 6241
Fax: 020-7437 6244
Acrylic, polyprop

Paint Creative 17 Holywell Hill,
St Albans, Herts, AL1 1EZ
Tel: 01727-836338
Fax: 01727-836099
Metallic and iridescent paints
and washes

Paul J Marks Mosaics
56 Hilda Road, Farnborough,
Orpington, Kent, BR6 7AW
Tel: 01689-850285
Fax: 01689-850285
Mosaic tiles

**Pentonville Rubber Products
Limited** 104/106 Pentonville Road,
London, N1 9LB
Tel: 020-7837 7553/4582
Fax: 020-7278 7392
Foam, rubber

Plasti-Kote London Road
Industrial Estate Sawston,
Cambridge, CB2 4TP
Tel: 01223-836400
Spray paints

Plotons 273 Archway Road,
Highgate, London, N6 5AA
Tel: 020-8348 0315
Fax: 020-8348 3414
Silver and gold transfer leaf,
acrylic size, brushes, fabric
paint, acrylic varnish

Selectasine
65 Chislehurst Road, Chislehurst,
Kent, BR7 5NP
Tel: 020-8467 8544
Mail order pigment colours

Stuart R. Stevenson,
68 Clerkenwell Road,
London, EC1M 5QA
Tel: 020-7253 1693
Fax: 020-7490 0451
Silver and gold transfer leaf,
acrylic size, brushes

Taw Glaziers
136 Fortis Green Road,
London, N10
Tel: 020-8883 7319
Glass, mirrors

The Bead Shop, 21a Tower Street,
Covent Garden, London, WC2 9NS
Tel: 020-7240 0931
Beads, beading thread, wire

The Cloth House 98 Berwick
Street, London, W1V 3PP
Tel: 020-7287 1555
and at 130 Royal College Street,
London, NW1 0TA
Tel: 020-7485 6247
An absolutely beautiful array of
fabrics from all over the world

The Mosaic Workshop
Unit B, 443-9 Holloway Road,
London, N7 6LJ
Tel: 020-7272 2446
Mosaic tiles

Wolfin Textiles Limited
64 Great Titchfield Street,
London, W1P 7AE
Tel: 020-7636 4949
Fax: 020-7580 4724
Email: cotton@wolfintextiles.co.uk
Website: www.wolfintextiles.co.uk
Linen, muslin, calico, cotton

Acknowledgements

I am very fortunate and privileged to have some special people in my life,
and even more so to be able to work with them. Work to me is fun: the
pleasure of creating something truly exciting with talented people makes
all the effort worthwhile. Life can't get much better.

The grand illusion of books is that the author does it all, but this is
actually a well-hidden untruth. There is a team of people that works tire-
lessly and patiently to make it what it is, all with an important role to play.

Emma and I would like to express our heart-felt thanks to all those people who have touched our lives and made this book possible and special.

Cindy Richards and Mark Collins: possessing vision is one thing, making it reality is another. Robin and Miranda, who have patience beyond
the call of duty. Paul Rolf, for tireless and unwavering energy. Without him
this book would simply not have been possible.

Featuring Kate Haxell, our secret ingredient. Lucinda Symons, who
adds her visionary eye to the proceedings. Brian Hatton, an unflappable
gentleman. Alistair Turnbull, for understanding our funny little ways. (Out
with hate, in with love.) Emma and Vicky, best prize for their supporting
role. Mima Cherry, even with a broken wrist this woman is unstoppable.
Juliet Maflin, wonderful catering, keeping us all going. This role can't be
underestimated, it is so important to keep the troops going. Margaret
Maflin, general gopher, you never get rid of your children!

Thank you to Vicky and Peter Farren, Andrew and Celia, Andrew
Hilton, Sarah, Peter, Katy, Gemma Robbins, Glen and Michelle, Stewart
and Sarah, Roger Oates for lending us the rug in the hall.

Index